HEAL

THROUGH

THE POWER OF

AWARENESS

DR. DENNIS MURPHY

Printed in the United States of America

First Printing, 2017

ISBN 978-1545410363

Falling Anvil Publishing

123 Mesa Street

Scottsdale, AZ 00000

www.TheNurturingDoctor.com

Book Design by Derek Murphy @creativindie

10 9 8 7 6 5 4 3 2 1

Dedication

In memory of Patrick Murray, S.A.C.
A mystic, a sage, a missionary, an educator, a profound
Presence and a good man.

To all the angels in my life. You know who you Are.

CONTENTS

PREFACE

If you suffer from depression, anxiety, addictions, anger, fear, obsessions, compulsions, phobias, poor health, unwanted behaviours and destructive relational patterns or if you feel unhappy, desperate, lost, alone or as if something very important in your life is missing; I hope you find healing from the words written in this book.

You are the reason this book was written.

In this book I lay down the ground work required for healing inner wounds. I reveal how inner wounds are created and what you can do to heal them. I explain how inner wounds from the long forgotten past are the cause of many of the difficulties experienced in present day life. I show how inner wounds are the driving force behind destructive behaviours, broken relationships, unhappiness, conflict, tumultuous emotions, addictions, depression, anxiety, anger, rage, fear, phobias, vindictiveness and violence.

I describe in detail the process of awareness which is the key to self knowledge and healing inner wounds. I discuss awareness as it pertains to all aspects of the human person including mind, emotions, body and Spirit. I also share my new groundbreaking insights which identify the root cause of mankind's deepest fear and show how this single factor creates so many of the problems that we experience in our daily lives. I have written the book in a way that nurtures your Spirit and begins the process of healing. This information will start you on the journey to healing your inner wounds and discovering a power within you that can change your life forever; so that you can begin living an exceptional life.

To understand how and why this book was written, come with me back in time to a beautiful spring morning in the centre of Canada. It seems like just yesterday. I was 23 years old. The bright sun and vivid blue sky enlivened my spirit and added to the excitement of the day. Inside the concert hall the spotlights, shining in my eyes, blinded me to the hundreds of people in the audience; as I anxiously walked to the centre of the stage.

There in front of me stood the recent Prime Minister of Canada. Prime Minister John George Diefenbaker congratulated me, shook my hand and presented to me my degree of Doctor of Veterinary Medicine. This moment marked the end of six long years of intensive study. What a day! What an experience!

After graduation a very good friend and I opened a veterinary clinic in Brandon, Manitoba and started using all the knowledge we had learned to care for the animals in the area. We provided care to all animals from horses to hamsters. My interest was in surgery and small animal medicine, although I loved getting out to the farms in the area to deliver calves, foals, lambs, kids (baby goats) and piglets and to treat all the various kinds of illnesses and disorders from which animals suffer. I enjoyed working with farmers and ranchers. I was using all my new knowledge and doing what I loved to do. Life could not get better than this!

So why, might you be wondering, is a veterinarian writing books on growth and healing inner wounds. Well, my life as a veterinarian was about to come to a sudden end. With what seemed like just a snap of the fingers, I lost everything. At the time, the doctors could not find the cause of what was making me so ill. I had a fever of 104°F for days on end. I had a headache so severe it felt like my head would explode. I was bedridden. Antibiotics did not help. It would only be many months later that I learned I had been stricken by two of the nasty zoonotic diseases which I had studied about in veterinary school. I had a meningoencephalitis, which simply means I had a brain infection. I never recovered from the damage caused by that illness.

It took me years to find my way out of the darkness and misery caused by this disease which I had caught from treating sick animals. I travelled the long journey from being a broken vet to being a whole person. At first, my goal was just to survive. The force behind this goal was more than just an instinctual drive and was very powerful. I was on the verge of death many times. I weighed 116 pounds. I had lost 60 pounds. I was quite literally skin and bones. I was a dead man walking.

To get well enough to enjoy life again meant gaining knowledge on how to heal myself. I had aided healing thousands of animals, but I did not know the first thing on how to heal myself. I suffered for many years and the steps to healing were slow and incremental. Healing not only involved changes in lifestyle and nutrition.

What amazed me was the power of the insights I experienced pertaining to my emotions, my body, my mind and my Spirit. Without these insights I would not be alive today. The insights were moments of clarity and connection which changed my emotional and mental programming. The insights had to do with reality and were not just intellectual facts and intellectual functioning. The insights saved my life.

When I look back over my life I can now see there was something much greater than myself, guiding me and helping me navigate through such difficult and treacherous times. I see the many miracles that happened in my life which have enabled me to be here today writing this book. I now enjoy life to the full. I am happy, deeply joyful and so full of gratitude for all that I am and for all that I have been given.

In this book and in my two upcoming books "Heal Through the Power of Being" and "Daily Bread", I share all the insights I have learned over my decades long journey from illness to life. It took suffering over many years to gain these insights.

I want to share these insights with you, so your journey to an exceptional life is shortened and so you can avoid as much suffering and damage as possible.

There is a very important point to highlight. If you have an illness such as diabetes, hypoglycemia, hormone imbalance, hypothyroidism, organic brain disease, poor health due to nutritional deficiencies, sickness from exposure to toxins, physical addictions to drugs or any other disorder seek medical help immediately. All the insights in the world will not prevent a panic attack caused by something as simple as caffeine addiction or hypoglycemia. The insights will help you live with these illnesses. The insights can help you heal the root causes of some of these types of problems, but immediate medical assessment and treatment for any physical or mental illness is imperative.

NOTE FROM AUTHOR

This book is about the way I connect to life. I'm sharing the insights I've gathered to offer a short cut on your journey to wisdom. The most important thing is how you see and connect with the world around you. You must look within, to connect with that which you sense as Life and Truth.

Do not be satisfied with an intellectual explanation or roadmap. Experience, enter into and live your life as fully as possible. This book attempts to describe that which is not able to be fully described in words. The intellect cannot be the master of your Essence. The intellect can only witness this magic and mystery within you... which *is* You. The intellect witnesses what Is. The intellect enters into what Is. There is so much more to you than your thoughts, emotions and behaviours.

Inner wounds which are composed of lies and pain and which are the result of having experienced lovelessness can and will blind you to the Truth about yourself, others and the Creator. Do not let these wounds rob you of your life and relationships. Do not let these wounds inflict further damage. Make the cycle stop here!

If what is written in this book resonates with Truth within you, then hold on to that Truth. Nurture your awareness of and connection to Truth. Learn to know Truth, and recognize it. You have that capacity deep within you. Truth must align with Love, Gentleness, Personhood, Presence, Peace, Reverence, Communion, Connection, Existence, Harmony, Autonomy and Amness. This is what I refer to as Being, Realities of Being, Center or Spirit. I invite you on this journey of awareness. Surrender to acceptance of your Self, as you are, here and now.

You are Accepted

CHAPTER ONE

Introduction

Awareness is a powerful process, but its simplicity makes it easy to overlook. The process of awareness is not complicated. Awareness is a gift that anyone can unwrap. It enables a person to grow in who they Are and Be who they Are. It enables healing of inner wounds.

Inner wounds and lack of awareness of who you Are,
block experiencing life to the full.

Inner wounds result from a lack of love and/or abuse—especially if experienced as a child. Awareness allows living life from a space of integration and harmony rather than from the automatic intellectual and emotional functioning associated with inner wounds and societal programming. Awareness shines a light on these automatic, unconscious, engrained and programmed ways of existing.

Awareness makes choice possible.

Awareness nurtures Presence in the moment. Awareness allows a new way of living. Awareness allows and nurtures Being. Being is Love, Life, Existence, Presence and Truth. Being is existing in and living from who you Are.

Being is existing in and living from
Love, Life, Presence, Existence and
All that is uniquely You.

When beginning the work and process of both healing inner wounds and reconnecting to Being, it is very important not to make any major changes or decisions in your life without first consulting a trusted professional, friends and/or family members. With that said, at times, drastic changes may be needed to allow and foster a safe and nurturing environment to heal, grow and Be. Trust what you sense deep within, beneath the turmoil created by emotions and intellectual imaginings.

Healing inner wounds is next to impossible without awareness of thoughts and emotions. Contrary to many common day beliefs, emotions need to be sensed, felt and expressed. This work of healing inner wounds from the past might seem exciting at first, but can also be intense, confusing and painful. Many inner wounds occurred during childhood, and unconsciously store pain and false beliefs in the body and mind. For this reason, the intellect can have a hard time coming to terms with intensely painful inner wounds. It is difficult for the intellect to make sense of this inner pain when the original trauma occurred years ago.

It takes time for the intellect to link the inner pain felt in the "present day" to the lovelessness experienced in childhood.

Unconscious emotions and false beliefs often cloud good judgment and decision-making. This confusion is a major cause of misplaced anger and aggression, as well as inappropriate and even violent behavior. Until the process of healing is understood, it's very important to seek sound advice from people who are safe, trusted and knowledgeable before making major decisions or lifestyle changes. If you suffer from inner wounds, the behavior and mannerisms of others can illicit strong emotional reactions within you.

Even insignificant interactions with others can cause major inner reactions.

These inner reactions can be inappropriately "acted out" causing harm to yourself and the people around you. A person with inner wounds often has inaccurate or distorted perceptions, especially when an inner wound becomes activated. Inner wounds can be activated by a number of triggers. Some common triggers are the behavior of others, the behavior of the person with inner wounds, the appearance and mannerisms of others, the appearance of self, illness, loss, aging, money matters, possessions and challenging life experiences or external events.

When inner wounds are triggered, out of proportion inner reactions include emotions that can range from elation and euphoria to sadness and deep depression. Examples of other emotions within this range are infatuation, craving, yearning, anger, rage, resentment, hate, fear, anxiety, panic, terror, horror, loneliness, emptiness, flatness, boredom, unhappiness, hopelessness, despair, desolation, despondency and numbness. Anger and fear are very common emotions associated with out of proportion reactions. Poor decisions are often made when experiencing intense and distracting emotions. These intense emotions cause the intellect to make erroneous assumptions and imagine all types of false scenarios. Poor decisions can have disastrous consequences and cause damage to self, others and relationships. Marriages can end, families can be broken, careers can be lost, people can be hurt, health can be undermined, and lives can be changed for the worse. Inner wounds resulting from lovelessness and abuse can wreak havoc in your life.

Inner wounds are usually unconscious.

Awareness is the solution.

Awareness brings a heightened understanding of intense emotion and distorted thinking. Awareness breaks the cycle of turmoil, alienation and isolation caused by inner wounds. Look for guidance and Presence on the journey to awareness, especially as you begin the work of healing and the painful emotions from the past start to surface. Do not act out the emotions or inner sensations in ways that hurt you, others, property or the environment.

You must become aware of your emotions and learn to

accept them. Feel your emotions and

express them safely.

Many people have suffered wounding of one kind or another. To be wounded means to have suffered a lack of love or an absence of love, especially as a child. To be wounded means to have been abused; either mentally, emotionally, physically or spiritually. Abuse combined with a lack or absence of love can create deeply painful inner wounds. Abuse is the extreme of lovelessness.

In your journey, you will meet people who are in touch with Being. They are precious gifts on the road of healing, but you must be ready to recognize them as valuable allies in confronting the inner pain and the untruth associated with inner wounds. Lack of love and abuse lead you to believe lies about yourself and others, which can distort your awareness. Inner wounds not only cloud perception but also block Being.

Awareness of Being is essential in
the work of inner healing.

It is only from the solidity of Being that you will be able to face the inner pain of abuse and confront the lies of lovelessness. Take the time to become aware of Being. If you want to begin the work of inner healing, work with safe and trusted mentors or friends who have travelled the road of healing or who have been on the road for some time. This is especially important when beginning the journey of healing. The Presence of others is a powerful way to awaken your intellect to your Presence within.

The Being of others touches the Love, Life, Existence,
Presence and Truth within you.

This is one way the intellect is awakened to the Reality of Being within. The intellect, body and emotions are awakened to Love, Life, Existence, Presence and Truth "within".

The Love of others awakens the Love "within".

In Being there is communion with self, others and God.

CHAPTER TWO

The Human Person:

*Body * Mind * Emotions * Spirit*

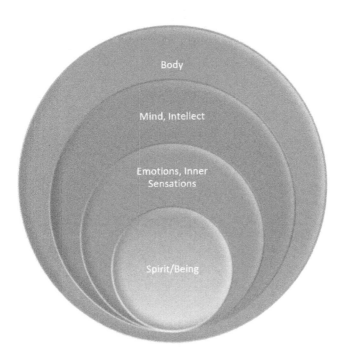

Whenever possible strengthen the awareness of

Life and the Truth of Life.

Enter Life. Exist in Life. Be.

What a miracle the human being is! How well we are made! Each of us is on such an amazing journey.

The "person" is created with the mind (intellect), the capacity for emotions, the body and the Spirit.

The mind, emotions, body and Spirit are all one and yet separate. Each facet of the **person** is a multitude of miracles in and of itself. I am in awe and wonder at the mystery and miracle of each person and of each person in relation to self, others, nature and the Author of all that is. May this book help to nurture and solidify personhood and the joy of life by increasing awareness, understanding and knowing of self (mind, body, emotions, Spirit) and by contributing to physical, mental, emotional and spiritual healing.

Personal growth and healing depends on each person's awareness of Being or Spirit. Quite simply, Being or Spirit means that Spark in a person, the Essence of a person which is expressed by their smile and mannerisms, the Amness of a person and the Twinkle in their eye. The Spirit is the Warmth, the Goodness, the Sacredness, the Uniqueness, the Presence and the Love in a person. The Spirit is that which is gone from the body once the body has died. Yet you can sense their Spirit in your heart if silently attentive.

No matter what your life circumstances or how traumatic your upbringing and life may have been, it is through awareness of Being you are made whole and are able to live life to the full.

Being is your Center.

In Being there is connection to self, others and the Creator. In Being there is acceptance of self. In Being you discover Truth. In Being you are "at one" with self and others.

Words are incapable of describing the wonder, reality, awe and power of Being. To know Being one must enter into Being. Ultimately all anyone has is Being. All else will pass. **Being is enough.** From Being life can truly be lived to the full. Although the intellect will try to convince you otherwise...

Being is Reality.

Know that within you, Being is real. Your work is to discover Being. Your work is to become aware of Being and enter into Being. Your work is to reconnect to Being. There is such Simplicity, Acceptance, Peace, Harmony, Lightness, Freedom, Uniqueness,

Completeness, Oneness and Wonder in Being. It is Being that fuels our mind and body. In Being we can accept and own our thoughts and emotions. In Being we are at one with all of self. Programming the intellect, emotions and body with the ways of lovelessness is what blocks Being.

A most important question to ask is "What is my relationship with myself in this present moment?" If I am not loving myself and in communion with myself in this now moment, am I then hating myself, rejecting myself, judging myself, condemning myself, negating myself, criticizing myself, ridiculing myself, tormenting myself with guilt, doubting myself and/or doubting my existence? In other words, am I not accepting myself, not wanting myself, not seeing myself, not believing myself, not protecting myself and/or not trusting myself? If so, is it possible to simply stop this inner "self" violence or at least begin to start recognizing this "self" rejection and "self" abuse?

The answer is yes! It is accomplished through awareness of all four facets of the human person. Awareness enables recognizing and identifying thoughts, emotions, inner sensations, body sensations and Realities of Being. Awareness leads to feeling and expressing the pain from wounds of lovelessness. Awareness leads to uncovering unconscious lies and self-destructive inner mechanisms. Most importantly, awareness leads to connecting to Being—that is, connecting to Love, Life and Truth within.

In Being there is no judgment; there is only Love. In Being there is Acceptance, Life, Existence, Peace, Presence, Gentleness, Harmony, Understanding, Oneness, Goodness, Wholeness, Compassion, Joy, Tenderness, Forgiveness, Communion, Connection and Amness. In

Being there is acceptance of and oneness with mind, emotions and body no matter what thoughts or emotions you experience.

In Being, there is a capacity for harmony
with mind, emotions and body.

From the strength and solidity of Being; all thoughts and emotions can be received, identified and processed. In Being there is Harmony and Autonomy and at the same time Connection and Communion.

Anxiety is the result of not having been loved enough; that is, not loved enough to be able to love yourself and not loved enough to simply Be, without needing to *Be More*. Love nurtures. Love protects. Love is Reality. Love is the medium of growth. Love permeates body, mind and emotions with Acceptance, Understanding, Worth, Preciousness, Recognition, Existence, Gentleness, Patience, Kindness, Truth, Solidity and Presence. Love resonates with Spirit. Anything else is based in lies or untruth. Anything else is the darkness, emptiness and agony of lovelessness. If you have not been loved enough to feel safe and secure, then your body, mind and emotions likely hold and create anxiety, pain and untruth.

What is Love? It is the answer to salvation, but we must seek it out. The task is to stop the inner self abuse and at the same time, find Truth and grow in Love.

The task is to discover and connect to the

Love, Life, Presence and Truth within.

To do this, we must recognize destructive patterns and inner wounds while reconnecting to Being... reconnecting to Love, Life, Existence and Truth within.

The task is to begin to Love self. Awareness of and connection to Being makes this possible.

To stop the inner violence and turmoil of self abuse you first have to "catch it"---to "recognize it". To catch it means to see what you are doing to yourself on the inside. The reason you abuse and reject yourself is because this is what you have been "taught" to do. To catch or see what you are doing to yourself, you need to be aware. Awareness is the key to self understanding and inner enlightenment. Attentiveness is the way which leads to awareness. Stillness and silence enable attentiveness.

Stillness and silence also bring you to your Center---to your Being. The Truth is within You. Love is within You. Let Love permeate your body, mind and emotions. Love is gentle. Love is kind. Love accepts. Love is patient. Love does not condemn. Love does not judge. Enter into Love. Enter into your Love within.

Be gentle with yourself. You Exist. You Are.

You are Good. You are Love.

Attentiveness is the mind becoming still; it's the mind turning away from distraction. In stillness and free from distraction the mind connects to Being. Attentiveness is the mind connecting to Being. You become Present to that to which you give your attention. Attentiveness is the process of becoming Present. The essence of Attentiveness is Presence. Attentiveness is becoming Present to your thoughts, body, emotions or Spirit Realities. Attentiveness is becoming Present to Others. Before you become Present to Others you need to become Present to Yourself. In Presence the intellect becomes attentive to thoughts, emotions, body or Spirit.

Lack of love can lead to self abuse and self rejection. Love is the medium in which we grow. A child needs to be "held" in Love. Love needs to saturate the mind, body and emotions. Love needs to be the way of Life. Love is about relationship—relationship with self and relationship with others. Love is about connection. Love nurtures and awakens the Love within. Love nurtures and awakens Being. Love is connection to self, to others and to God.

Awareness of Being takes time, patience and perseverance if a person has suffered years of abuse and lovelessness as a child.

Experiencing abuse and lovelessness as an adult can also blind a person to the awareness of Being. The solution is to *feel your feelings.*

Feeling your feelings opens you to your inner world. The more you feel your feelings the less you will be afraid of them. You can "Be" with all your feelings. Your feelings will shine a light on the mechanisms of inner self abuse. Your feelings will shine a light on the core lies you believe. Your feelings are the body's way of drawing attention to that which is unprocessed. Your feelings are your inner reactions to unconscious self destructive mechanisms, inner pain and unconscious lies you believe about yourself.

Inner self abuse is a "learned" pattern of relating to self. It is a result of experiencing lovelessness and abuse, especially as a child.

Awareness, Love, Acceptance, Gentleness, Patience, Presence and Compassion are necessary to dismantle these unconscious learned abusive patterns of relating to self. Awareness of thoughts and feelings leads to awareness of the learned unconscious inner self abuse mechanisms. Once you are aware of the "inner" self abuse, such as self rejection, you can **acknowledge** it. To acknowledge means to recognize, to own and to admit. Acknowledgment requires **openness** and **humility**.

Humility is not humiliation. Humility is accepting "what is" with gentleness and understanding and with no judgment. Let your feelings BE. Let your feelings come. Let your feelings guide you to express what needs to be expressed...to express what is stored within.

Let your feelings express themselves through your body,

in a safe and non hurtful manner.

This process will lead to awareness of inner wounds and specific aspects and mechanisms of inner self abuse. Once you are aware of and have acknowledged an inner mechanism of self abuse, such as self rejection or self hate, you can now **catch it**. Awareness of the problem allows you to make a deliberate decision. You can choose to stop this inner self abuse and self rejection. You can choose to say "NO" to self rejection or self hate. If the patterns of self abuse and self rejection are **deeply engrained** it may be necessary to choose to accept, for now, that you are not able to stop it. Just the "recognition" of inner self abuse is a huge step. Acceptance of "what is" brings inner peace and harmony.

As awareness of Being grows, the choice between self rejection and self acceptance becomes possible and easier. It is made possible by turning away from the automatic learned self rejection and self judgment and returning to the Truth of your Spirit. It is made possible by awareness of the lies fuelling the patterns of self abuse and self rejection. In Being there is no judgment, rejection or hate. In Being there is Acceptance, Peace, Gentleness, Understanding, Tolerance, Patience and Love. In Being you can acknowledge and accept inner mechanisms such as judgment, rejection and hate. Acceptance does not mean to condone. Acceptance leads to and allows acknowledgment.

Acceptance enables choice. Choice empowers.

Choice is liberating.

You can begin to say no to self rejection and other forms of self abuse. You have this power. It takes gentle non judgmental attentiveness and patience to become aware of the different inner mechanisms of self abuse. At times it is necessary to wait for light and Truth and live with the uncomfortable. Awareness will come. Awareness enables you to make a decision. Awareness gives you a choice.

Know that Love has nothing to do with judging, rejecting, hating, berating, negating, condemning, not wanting or not accepting yourself. Love has nothing to do with guilt.

To stop abusing and rejecting yourself you also need to catch the unconscious lies about yourself which you have been led to believe and taught to believe are truth. Awareness allows you to catch unconscious lies. The lies fuel self abuse and self rejection. The lies justify and enforce this learned, engrained, automatic and most often unconscious self abuse and self rejection. Lovelessness and the pain of lovelessness spawn these lies.

With awareness comes the ability to make a choice. Once you make a choice to *stop* it—that is, stop judging yourself, hating yourself, rejecting yourself, condemning yourself, negating yourself, beating yourself, criticizing yourself, doubting yourself, ridiculing yourself, putting yourself down and believing lies—you can choose to replace this externally learned inner self abuse with seeing yourself (seeing your

Spirit, your goodness, your worth, your personhood), accepting yourself, wanting yourself, believing yourself, understanding yourself, hearing yourself and being gentle with yourself. Further you can choose the Truth of your Spirit, that is the Truth of your Amness, Existence, Presence, Personhood, Worth and Goodness even in the face of others rejecting you, hating you or abusing you.

Others rejecting, hating and abusing you triggers self negating and self destroying unconscious lies. These lies are learned, engrained, automatic and unconscious. Awareness brings consciousness to this hidden source of agony and destructiveness. Awareness brings light to this darkness. This is what working out your salvation means.

I Am, You Are, Love Is.

These words proclaim Reality.

Whether you know it or not, feel it or not and understand it or not; God, Supreme Being, The Creator, Yahweh, Allah, Higher Power, Jesus—whatever attempt is made to name this indescribable "ISNESS"—loves you and loves you beyond comprehension. The fact that You Are means you are Loved. Within you, is this connection and communion.

The most powerful way to receive and come to know

this Truth and this Reality,

is to be still.

In Being you will come to know this Truth and Reality to the depths of your mind, body and feelings. Silence and stillness lead to Being. Thoughts and feelings do not negate Being. The intellect or mind needs to quiet itself and simply observe this Reality within. When the mind is quiet it has a chance to become aware of this inner Reality.

You can "Be".

The mind can become one with Being.

The mind connects to Being.

The mind is absorbed by Being.

Whatever your thoughts, beliefs, feelings or even what others may say about you; there are absolutely no exceptions: **You are Loved. Love is within You.** No matter what you may have done, what you may have not done, what you look like, what things you have or do not have, what you do, what happens to you, what people may say or think about you, what amount of money you have or don't have and on and on... You are Loved. You are accepted, seen, wanted, heard and received.

You...Exist. You...Are. Your Being...Is.

You do not have to earn Love. You do not have to perform to get Love. You do not have to *"do"* anything to achieve Love. Quite simply, Love Is. You have always been loved and always will be loved. Love is within You. You are Love. Enter into Love. This can be a difficult reality to grasp for those who have experienced lovelessness and abuse.

God is within you and you are within God. After years of searching, this is my experience. This reality has been within me all along. If it is true for me, then it is surely true for you. You are made in the "image and likeness" of God...of Love. Stop...be still...and wonder at this amazing Truth. Become one with this Reality. At the very depths of you is your Spirit, your Center, your Essence, your Being. This is who you really Are. You Exist. You are Love, Life and Truth. The kingdom of God (your Being) is **within you.** Within your Being you are connected to Yahweh...to the great I Am. The **Truth** will set you **free.** Do not demand God's love.

Just be still and let God Be for God is Love.

If you have suffered lovelessness and abuse it may take some time to experience and become aware of this Reality. Be Patient. Be gentle with yourself. No judgment. Accept yourself.

Within this discussion it is important to clarify God is not a god of judgment, rejection, condemnation, hate, wrath, punishment, guilt or negation. The word I have grown to love when referring to God is the word...Yahweh. When translated it means "I Am." The great "I Am." Words betray me when attempting to convey this Presence that

I so very strongly sense and connect to within. It has been a long road to this awareness. I hope these writings can awaken your intellect to this connection within you.

Suffering points us towards home. It leads us back to our Center, our Spirit, our Essence. It points us home to Being, to Truth and to the Now. Suffering can be the result of naturally occurring events, life events, tragedies, disasters, our own choices, others abusing us, unmet childhood needs, unmet adult needs and unconscious lies. The pain we experience from whatever the cause can be a doorway leading us to our Essence. The pain can alert us to the need to reconnect to Being, to heal from inner wounds, to become aware of unconscious lies we believe, to change our thinking patterns and attitudes, to process our emotions, to face our life, to live our life and to become aware of how we relate to self, to others and to God. Suffering motivates us to heal and to come home to Being. Suffering can lead us to Being. Suffering can lead us to existing.

Emotions and inner sensations lead us to awareness of inner pain. We need to become aware of the pain. We need to become aware of the cause of the inner pain we experience. To do this it is necessary to be attentive to the story the pain is revealing. At the same time and most importantly, it is necessary to become aware of Spirit and aware of Existence; which is awareness of Love, Life, Presence and Truth "within."

Whether you are "overly" anxious, sad, depressed, angry or elated; these emotions or states of living are often a sign and opportunity to heal. These inner reactions are doorways to healing. Healing involves awareness of unconscious lies, feeling and expressing pain, awareness of the Truth and Reality of Being and existing in choosing the Truth and choosing Being. Unconscious lies can be lies or untruths about yourself, others and God. Lies can be about negating yourself and even negating your very existence. Lies can involve false beliefs concerning your source, that is, from where you get your life and existence.

Being is not just a concept or some intellectual idea. Being is not fictional. Being is within each person. Being is a reality. Being is *the* Reality. Being is what you must come to **know**...come to know in the depths of your mind, body and emotions. Come deeper into Being. Enter Being. Enter Amness. Enter Now.

No matter what you have done or not done, no matter who loves you or doesn't love you, no matter if everyone rejects you or hates you, no matter if you do not love yourself or even if you reject and hate yourself... you Exist, you Are. In the face of the pain and the lies, come back to Truth and to Reality. Come back to "*I Am.*" Come back to the Truth and the Reality that...

I Am, You Are, Love Is.

CHAPTER THREE

Awareness

Connecting with Your Mind, Emotions, Body and Spirit.

Awareness is your mind connecting to you...all of you!

Awareness is simply your mind, that is your intellect, connecting to you. Awareness is your mind connecting to all of you, but most importantly, connecting to "who you Are" in your Essence. Awareness is the mind connecting to what you experience "within" yourself. Awareness is the process of becoming connected in the present moment with your thoughts, your emotions, your inner sensations, your body and your Spirit. Awareness is the process of becoming **conscious.**

The most profound and life changing level of awareness is the mind awakening to the Reality of Being.

Awareness is consciousness. Awareness enables you to become conscious of your thoughts, emotions, inner sensations, beliefs, attitudes, body and Spirit. Becoming conscious is not some mysterious experience for only mystic sages or the enlightened few. Consciousness is for every human being. It is simply the process of getting to **know** your "self". It is the process of coming to know *"who You Are"* and to really know that *"You...Are"*. You **Are,** You **Exist**...with all your thoughts, all your emotions and all your body...and that is good, and that is okay. *No judgment!* You are Spirit with all your thoughts, emotions and body.

The deepest level of consciousness is connection to the Reality of Being...to "I Am".

Awareness calls for an attitude of openness, gentleness, humility, acceptance and no judgment. Awareness requires attentiveness to thoughts, emotions, the body and to Being or Spirit Realities. Attentiveness is the inner act of standing back in gentle stillness in the present moment and shifting your attention to what you think, what you feel, what you sense in your body or to who you Are in your

Essence. You simply observe your thoughts, emotions, body or Spirit Realities. Being present to, that is, being attentive to thoughts, emotions, body or Spirit leads to awareness. With practice you will be able to identify thoughts, learn the language of your emotions, sense the wisdom of your body and connect to your Spirit. With awareness of thoughts, emotions, body and Spirit Realities it is possible to acknowledge you...all of "You". To acknowledge is to own and to admit "what is".

Become present to your thoughts, emotions and body. Acknowledge...your thoughts...your emotions...and your body...with an attitude of Acceptance, Gentleness, Openness, Humility, Truth, Love and no judgment. Acknowledge these Realities of Being. Through this in-depth awareness and acknowledgement it is possible to *accept*. It is possible to make a *choice* to accept. **Accept all of you.** Through awareness you can acknowledge the *resistance* to accept all of you.

With acceptance you can even accept that "you are not able to accept".

Acceptance enables you to accept resistance and confusion. Acceptance confounds the intellect. Acceptance is from your Spirit. It is fluid, peaceful, open, gentle, kind, understanding, non-judgmental and non-violent. Acceptance enables us to be at ease within. Acceptance creates harmony. Acceptance heals alienation, division and isolation. Acceptance allows unity and integration "within".

Acceptance leads to the state of being "at one" with self and with others. Through acceptance you can acknowledge "what is". With acceptance you turn away from self judgment and self rejection. Self judgment and self rejection are functions of the intellect and ego.

Acceptance is not resignation. Acceptance is the letting go of denial. Acceptance is the shift from self rejection and self judgment to Being. Acceptance is from your Spirit. Shift from your intellect or ego to your Spirit. Shift from self rejection and self judgment to Acceptance.

You can do this even with the echoes of self rejection and self judgment vibrating in your feelings.

Awareness is the realization of "what is". Acknowledgment is the process of allowing the realization of "what is". Acknowledgment is the act of admitting "what is". Acknowledgment is the act of owning "what is". Acceptance is the realization, recognition and owning of "what is" with no judgment. *Acceptance is the sense of "what is...is".* Acceptance is about acceptance of self with no judgment.

Acceptance has to do with no judgment of self and no judgment of thoughts, emotions, inner sensations, body and Spirit Realities.

Acceptance is an act of deep Love. Acceptance is about accepting the person, that is, accepting "you" and accepting the reality of what is. Acceptance nurtures and enables "in-depth awareness" of unconscious thoughts, emotions, inner sensations, beliefs and attitudes. Acceptance provides safety and security. Acceptance holds the person in Love. There is no rejection, hatred, judgment, condemnation, negation, criticism, shaming, threats or punishment in Acceptance. Acceptance is the Presence of Love. Only through Acceptance and Openness can you become aware of inner wounds. Through Acceptance you begin to heal. ***Acceptance is from Being.*** Acceptance provides an environment "within", which enables in-depth awareness. Acceptance is an act of loving yourself. Acceptance and acknowledgment are closely linked inner processes. As you acknowledge, you at the same time begin to accept.

Be aware that lovelessness programming can deeply engrain unconscious attitudes and mechanisms of self rejection, self judgment, self condemnation and self hate. Be patient, gentle, kind and understanding with yourself. Persevere. Awareness will give you the keys to free yourself from this prison. The process takes time. The process involves shifting from these destructive mechanisms to the way of the Spirit, which is the way of Reality...the way of Love. Anything else is based in lies and lovelessness.

To summarize, the process of awareness can be teased apart into four separate realities. These four realities nurture and pave the way to connection and communion with self. The four realities are connected to Being. The four realities are:

HEAL THROUGH THE POWER OF AWARENESS

1) Attentiveness and Presence
2) Awareness or Realization
3) Acknowledgement
4) Acceptance

Attentiveness leads to awareness. Attentiveness involves your mind connecting to your Presence. The mind becomes still and silent. The mind enters stillness and silence in the present moment. The mind, in the Presence of Being, is then attentive to either thoughts, emotions, inner sensations, the body or Spirit Realities. The mind is open to what is sensed *within*. The mind is open to "what is" within. Attentiveness to thoughts, emotions, body or Spirit leads to **awareness** of thoughts, emotions, body or Spirit. Emotions and inner sensations are sensed in the body. With awareness you can **acknowledge**. Through awareness and acknowledgement, **acceptance** is possible.

At the actual point of awareness the mind can tear apart from Being and begin to judge, hate, reject and/or condemn the awareness and/or self. This is the ego part of the mind trying to protect itself. The ego is the part of the mind that is unable to face core lies and inner pain. The mind created the ego in the void of lovelessness. The lack of "awareness of" and "connection to" Being together with inner pain and untruth create this void...this sense of nothingness within. The ego part of the intellect does not want to confront this inner void. Inner pain, untruth and lack of connection to Being are the result of lovelessness. Without "awareness of" and "connection to" Being, the mind creates the ego as a way to survive. What else can the mind do? The mind on its own cannot face non-Being, that is, non-existence. More accurately, the mind on its own cannot face the "lie" of non-Being.

The mind through the ego can judge, reject, hate and condemn the newly realized thoughts, emotions, inner sensations, body insights and/or Spirit Realities. Most often the mind rejects, judges, hates and/or condemns "self" for having such thoughts, emotions, inner sensations, body insights, attitudes and beliefs. Lovelessness; especially when experienced as a child; programs the mind to reject, judge, hate and/or condemn.

Lovelessness creates deep-seated core lies and inner pain which fuel both the mind's imaginings and destructive mechanisms.

Without judging self, the mind can turn away from lovelessness programming; that is, turn away from the ego, and stay connected to Being...connected to Acceptance, Understanding, Gentleness, Compassion, Openness, Tolerance, Patience and Love. Connected to Being, any new awareness can be received and embraced without judgment, hate, rejection and condemnation of self or the awareness. In fact, connected to Being, any new awareness can be received and embraced in the face of all the learned, automatic and psychologically entrenched judgment, hate, rejection and condemnation. "Be with" a new awareness whatever it may be. At the same time be with the engrained self rejection and self judgment. Remember...You Are. You Exist.

With awareness and an attitude of no judgment the choice to accept all of you is a natural progression because the intellect comes to realize and to see that *"what is...Is"*. The intellect sees the wisdom of connecting to Acceptance. There is Peace, Autonomy, Oneness and Harmony in Acceptance. There is a moment when the intellect stops the inner fighting, denial, suppression and repression. There is a moment when the intellect sees it can survive the awareness and that reality does not mean death or non-existence. There is no longer denial or suppression of what is. Let go of denying and suppressing thoughts and emotions. Acceptance allows and embraces all inner reactions. You do not even have to like "what is". "I might not like 'what is' but that is how it is." **In other words, acceptance can accept non-acceptance.** You can accept your non-acceptance. Acceptance is the peace giving process of surrendering to and admitting that "what is...Is".

Acceptance does not mean "acting out" of thoughts and emotions. Do not "act out" of any new awareness concerning thoughts and emotions in a way that is harmful to yourself or others. Allow, receive and embrace the awareness of your thoughts and emotions but, as intense and tumultuous as emotions can be, do not act out of the emotions in ways that are hurtful or destructive to others or their property.

As sure as emotions come,

emotions will also fade away.

With awareness, "acceptance" becomes a choice. In the present moment, accept you are Spirit and accept your emotions, your thoughts and your body. Accept You. ***Once you learn to accept yourself you can accept others***. It is okay not to be perfect. It is okay to make mistakes. It is okay to be confused. With Acceptance come Peace, Connection, Communion, Harmony and Oneness within yourself and with all.

You and Your Behaviour

The goal of the work of awareness is to begin living your life to the full by both healing inner wounds and connecting to Being. During this work of healing inner wounds, intense thoughts and emotions can surface. This fact makes it critically important to discuss behavior. Inner wounds are core lies and inner pain, either alone or in combination.

Destructive and violent behavior is driven by unconscious core lies and unconscious inner pain. The core lies and inner pain have a variety of causes, all of which are discovered through awareness. The most common causes of core lies and inner pain are lovelessness, abuse, major losses, untruth and traumatic life events; especially when experienced as a child.

The core lies create intense and powerful emotions.
The inner pain in itself is an intense
and powerful emotion.

These types of emotions are often repressed resulting in surface emotions like anger, rage and fear. Even these surface emotions can be repressed or stuffed creating feelings of anxiety, sadness, numbness, flatness and depression. These unconscious emotions still drive and fuel behavior. Sadly, without awareness, intense emotions like rage, fear and depression can lead to destructive, addictive and violent behaviors damaging people, families and relationships.

Until getting to the stage of healing, behavior must be managed. This is especially the case if powerful emotions begin to surface. *Do not behave or act in a way that hurts yourself, others or property.* This is the number one guideline when managing your behavior and doing the work of awareness and healing. Leave the situation before you act out of intense emotions in a violent or destructive way.

Acceptance and Destructive Behaviour

Growth is possible through awareness, acknowledgment and acceptance. You are not able to make a choice without these three steps. This leads to the subject of destructive or hurtful behavior. **You do not need to accept your destructive behavior but that does not mean** *you do not accept "you".* You do need to accept the reality of your behavior or the reality of the pattern of your behavior, even destructive behaviour. Acknowledgement and acceptance are closely interwoven.

You acknowledge and accept your destructive behavior without self judgment or self rejection. This does not mean you condone such behavior in the sense of letting yourself repeat these behaviours. *You can judge and reject destructive behavior but do not judge and reject you.* Become aware of destructive behavior and stop destructive behavior by managing this behavior. Learn to manage destructive behavior. To heal, use these behaviours to become aware of the inner forces and inner mechanisms driving these same destructive behaviours.

Destructive behaviours are usually triggered by external events. How does this happen? It happens because external events trigger powerful emotions associated with inner wounds. The natural tendancy is to act out of these powerful and intense emotions. *Turn away from destructive behaviours and shift your focus inward to what you experience, feel or sense within.* Work with these inner forces; to heal inner pain and uncover core lies and self destructive inner mechanisms. Shift your attention inwards. Work with your feelings. Work with your emotions and inner sensations. Be attentive to these inner vibrations. Become open and vulnerable to what is happening within you. *Let yourself be affected by your emotions and inner sensations.*

To summarize, your behavior is not who you Are. *Your behavior is not your thoughts, emotions, body or Being.* Behaviour is an action. Behaviour is often a symptom. Acceptance is not about condoning destructive behavior, abuse, untruth and lovelessness. You can accept everything sensed "within". It is important to acknowledge and accept everything sensed within. This does not mean you "act on" or "act out" everything sensed "within". Also, this does not mean you condone everything sensed within. *"You" are always acceptable. The person is always acceptable.* All your thoughts, all your emotions, all of your body and your Being are acceptable. It is the person's behavior that is not always acceptable. *Do not behave or act in a way that hurts yourself, others or property.* This is a simple guide to use as you become aware of new thoughts, beliefs, memories, emotions and inner sensations. You can choose whether or not to act out of thoughts and emotions once you realize the difference between "processing" your thoughts and emotions and "acting out" of your thoughts and emotions. Without this awareness learn to manage your behavior so as not to hurt yourself, others or relationships.

It is important to acknowledge "what is". Do not jump over the truth of..."what is". Why do I say this? Because most often, you cannot heal what you do not acknowledge. Having said that, awareness of Being is very profound and powerful. Awareness of Being is the power that heals mind, body and emotions. "Being" does not follow rules set up by the intellect.

Acceptance and Core Lies

Acceptance of self does not mean acceptance of believed core lies in the sense that a believed core lie is okay. Core lies are not okay. You are okay. You, believing the lie because of lack of awareness, are okay. But the lie is not okay. The lie is damaging. 'I am bad', 'I am not good enough', 'I am not important', 'I am nothing', 'I am no good', 'I am of no worth', 'I do not exist' and 'I am not' are examples of core lies. You need to accept and acknowledge that you believe the lie. If you do not, the lie will stay repressed or hidden in the unconscious and continue to deny you your life.

If you could "see" the lie and "see" the Truth, you would choose the Truth. You would automatically believe the Truth because the Truth is the deepest part of you. Core lies are destructive. The person is acceptable. You are acceptable. The person believing core lies because of lack of awareness is acceptable. Work at becoming aware of the core lies you believe. **Awareness weakens the core lie's hold on you.** At the same time, nurture connection to Being. Being is Reality and Truth.

Remember, you believe core lies because that is what you have been taught to believe.

Further, acceptance means if for now you cannot see the Truth, then that is how it is. What is...is. Be very gentle and patient with yourself at times like this. Core lies are a result of suffering lovelessness and abuse. **Lovelessness and abuse engrain core lies.** As a child you needed Love, Connection and Presence; not lovelessness, alienation and abuse. The core lie is destructive and will affect thoughts, emotions and behavior. The lie is evil. The person believing the lie is not evil. The lie has nothing to do with the identity and deep reality of the person.

The core lie is just that...a lie. The person is Good. The person is Sacred. You are Good. You are Sacred. The person, believing the core lie, is trapped because of both the lack of awareness of the lie and, more importantly, the lack of awareness of Self...the lack of awareness of Love, Presence and Truth within.

Core lies and inner pain can fuel destructive behavior. Behaviour can be judged using the phrase "what is the most loving thing to do" as a guide post. Often we miss the mark of living by this guide. Destructive behaviour is a symptom of the deeper problem of believed core lies and inner pain. The person is not the problem. There needs to be separation between the person and the person's behavior. The Spirit of the person is good. Core lies, inner pain, lack of connection to Being and mental dysfunction are at the root of destructive behavior. It is vitally important to learn to manage destructive behavior if you do not know how to safely process intense emotions. Seek out a trusted person to receive you and lead you through this process.

Once we lose sight of the "person" all is lost. Believed core lies resulting from abuse and lovelessness are persistent. It takes time to purge these lies from the body, mind and emotions. Awareness of the core lie and at the same time awareness of Truth and Love within are the answer to dispelling inner core lies.

This is the fine line of separation. Separation is the process of separating Truth from untruth. Separation leads to inner clarity. As discussed, a person's behavior may be "bad". The person's actions may be "bad". *The person is not bad.* What is bad and evil are the unconscious core lies. The person may be lost but *the person is good.* To move forward it is necessary to accept the reality of such behavior.

Separate the person from the behavior. Separate yourself from your behavior.

Destructive actions and behaviors, fuelled by attitudes and beliefs based in lies and lovelessness, have consequences; whether a person is aware or not. Believed core lies are destructive and can result in destructive behavior. These facts make awareness and healing so very important. Let go of self rejection, self hate, self condemnation and self judgment. Be patient with yourself. Be Compassionate, Understanding, Gentle, Accepting and Tolerant with yourself. You are Good. You are important. You Are. Do not judge yourself.

While on the subject of separation it is important to discuss feelings. *Feelings are often judged as bad.* Feelings of anger, rage, resentment, hatred, depression, pain, wanting to be destructive or even wanting to be violent are often judged as bad or wrong. More importantly, the person having these feelings can mistakenly be judged as bad or wrong. Feelings are not bad or wrong.

The person having the feelings is not bad or wrong or defective or a failure, no matter what the feelings are.

"Acting out" in ways that are destructive or violent towards self, others or property, because of what you think or feel, is what can be judged as bad and wrong. Judging feelings or the person for having the feelings leads to denying and repressing feelings. Denying and repressing feelings leads to "acting out" of feelings. Feelings need to be recognized, acknowledged, accepted and then "processed" safely and constructively. The intellect is an expert at jumping over, ignoring, denying and repressing feelings. Slow your thinking. Become still. Shift your attention to within. Become attentive to your feelings.

Awareness is not only the process of hearing and understanding unconscious thoughts, beliefs, attitudes, emotions and inner sensations. Awareness is also the process which leads to connection to Being. With awareness, acknowledgement and acceptance, it is possible to know, to see, to hear and to experience...*I Am*...*You Are*...and **Love Is**. Awareness is the light of your inner world. It is a gift and the key to Reality...to Truth...to Love...to Being. Knowing Reality is consciousness. Consciousness is an amazing journey. It can be the longest journey you will ever take and yet it is only a few inches long! It is the journey within. It is the journey from your head to your heart and then to your Center...to your Being. Your heart is the awareness of and connection to Being.

Guard your heart. It is your heart that can be broken.

Being can never be broken.

Awareness is simple but takes time, practice, patience and some work. The pay off or reward is inner Clarity, coming to know yourself, coming to see yourself, coming to understand yourself, coming to accept yourself, Autonomy, Inner Space, Connection, Communion, Peace, Oneness, Healing, Freedom, Truth, Wholeness and Harmony. Awareness leads to freedom from untruth, core lies, alienation, isolation, division, self judgment, self rejection, self hate and self condemnation. It is an exciting process and it has everything to do with You. It is about your Life and what makes you tick! Once you begin this journey, it is difficult to turn back. So, how do you do it? Let's get on with that...with becoming aware of your thoughts, emotions, body and Spirit.

CHAPTER FOUR

Awareness of Thoughts & Intellect

Remember...just because you "think" something does not make it true.

Further...just because you "believe" something does not make it true.

Awareness of thoughts or thinking has to do with the mind or intellect. Awareness of thoughts includes conscious and unconscious thoughts, beliefs and attitudes. Thoughts, beliefs and attitudes can be based in truth or untruth. Thought awareness is an easy to learn yet powerful tool. You can change your life by changing your thoughts. You change your thoughts by becoming aware of your thoughts and then choosing thoughts or thinking patterns based in Truth and Reality.

The process involves consciously shifting your focus to your thoughts so you can "see" what your thoughts say, in other words, to see what *you* are thinking! For the most part, the mind rambles on, thinking without being aware of individual thoughts. We think automatically with most thoughts not even registering in consciousness.

To test this, try speaking out loud all the thoughts you think. Remember no judgment of your thoughts or of yourself for having the thoughts. This exercise will also start you on the process of developing the skill of thought awareness. Many thoughts have been programmed into us over a number of years. Also, the inner base which fuels many thoughts has been programmed into us over many years. The programming comes from parents, family, friends, church, society, the media, academic institutions, writings, advertising, our self, body language, relationships, events, experiences and a myriad of other sources. Most thoughts are automatic and unconscious, but if you become aware of your thoughts you can learn to choose what you think. Also, you can change not only what you think but you can change your attitudes and what you believe.

The first step in learning the skill of thought awareness is to slow down thoughts and thinking by becoming *present* in the now moment. Forget about what is going on out there...outside of you. Take your attention off the *external* situation and events. Take your attention off people, behavior, situations or events which may be affecting you.

Shift your attention from without to "within".

Take a couple of deep breaths to become present in the moment. Then become attentive to what you are actively but most likely unconsciously thinking. Simply observe your thoughts. Observe what is going through your mind at this moment...in this present moment. *Discover* what is going on in your mind. Watch your thoughts and write them down as they come and go. Do not deny, suppress, ignore or distract yourself from any thoughts. Just let them be.

Do not judge your thoughts and do not judge yourself for having them. You are *not* your thoughts. Judging your thoughts or yourself will only suppress your thoughts or cause you to unconsciously deny them. Becoming aware of your thoughts is the first step in managing them. You will not be able to manage your thoughts if you are not aware of what you are thinking. Again, thoughts are very fast and often we are unaware of what our thoughts are saying. It is important to reiterate that judging yourself or your thoughts only drives thoughts deeper into the unconscious.

Practice several times a day just observing your thoughts. Practice becoming conscious of your thoughts. *Do not act out of inappropriate thoughts.* Do not get caught up in the content or meaning of your thoughts. Just let your thoughts come and go. Stand back from your thoughts and just observe them. Observe what your thoughts are saying. Observe the Love and Truth they are expressing, the claims they are making, the facts they are preaching, the assumptions they are stating, the conclusions they are declaring, the beliefs they are asserting, the emotions they are communicating, the fantasies they are describing and the judgments they are proclaiming. Whatever your thoughts, see them as just thoughts.

Do not act out of them or get lost in them, as tempting as this can be. Only stand back and observe them.

It is often helpful to write down what your thoughts say. Remember...be gentle with yourself and no judgment. If you find it difficult to identify thoughts, practice recognizing your thoughts when you are alone and in a quiet place. Think of a recent or future situation, encounter, event or experience. Let yourself be in that situation and allow any emotions to well up within you. Try to identify your thoughts as you think of the incident. What thoughts are triggered in you by the remembered incident? What are your thoughts in response to the incident?

An example could be thoughts concerning a job interview. Some thoughts might be "I can't do this interview!", "What will these people think about me?", "I answered the questions poorly.", "I am not dressed well enough.", "I am going to botch this interview.", "I am not good enough to be hired.", "There is nothing good about me.", "They won't hire me!", "I never get amazing jobs.", "There are other people so much better than I.", etcetera. Thoughts like this are fast, automatic and often unconscious.

For now just practice becoming aware of your thoughts. Remember your thoughts are just thoughts. Your thoughts are **not** who you are. Your thoughts may be true or untrue.

With awareness of what your thoughts say, you can begin to ask if your thoughts are based in Truth. By doing this, you are challenging your thoughts. Just becoming aware of what your thoughts say will give you an inner shift and a sense of "ahhh, so that is what I am thinking". This awareness of your thoughts may lead to the realization..."no wonder I feel like I do, if that is what I think and believe".

To summarize the example, the first incremental step is just the awareness of the thought or awareness you have a thought in response to the situation. Following this is the awareness of what the thought is saying..."I can't do this...I just can't do this".

The following steps in the process of thought awareness are helpful:

1. Stop....whatever situation you are in just....Stop. Stop and become *still* within.

2. Take a few deep breaths. Become *present*. Become present in the *moment*. Become present to yourself in the moment in whatever the circumstances may be.

3. Ask yourself, "What am I thinking right now...at this moment...in this situation?"

4. Gently focus on what you are thinking. Be attentive to your thoughts.

5. Let the thoughts BE no matter what they are. Just acknowledge and name them. Identify them. Let them come and go. You may find it helpful to write them down. This slows down your thoughts and your thinking.

6. *No judgment*. This is very important. No judgment of your thoughts and especially *no judgment of yourself* for having the thoughts, no matter what the thoughts are. You are okay, you

are acceptable, you are good, you are of worth, you Are...no matter what your thoughts are.

7. *Do not act out of inappropriate thoughts.* Do not let inappropriate thoughts guide your behavior or actions.

8. Challenge your thoughts by asking if your thoughts are the truth. Do not just let your thoughts have their way with you! Replace any thoughts based in untruth with the Truth.

Thoughts are often layered. Some thoughts are superficial and other thoughts are deeper in the unconscious. Both these types of thoughts can occur at the same time. The superficial thoughts often distract from or blur the deeper, more unconscious thoughts. In the above example of the job interview the more superficial thoughts deal with things like "Is my hair combed?", "Do I have all my resource papers?", "Where is the interview?", or "Do I have enough time to make the interview?" The deeper, more unconscious thoughts are often associated with your abilities, your weaknesses and your perceived identity. These deeper types of thoughts connect to the next level of awareness, which is awareness of feelings.

As thought awareness grows it leads to the next step in self awareness which is the awareness of feelings. Awareness of feelings is the process of learning to identify emotions and inner sensations. Awareness of emotions and inner sensations goes deeper into the unconscious.

The content of emotions and inner sensations reveals inner wounds, core lies, beliefs, attitudes and even leads full circle back to unconscious thoughts.

We often believe our thoughts automatically. Do not let this happen. It is worth repeating. Thinking or believing a thought does not make it true. *You do not have to believe your thoughts. Also, you do not have to believe your beliefs.* Acknowledge the discovery of any thoughts or beliefs you believe as true. Do not judge yourself for any conscious or unconscious thoughts or beliefs you discover. Do not judge yourself for believing these thoughts or beliefs. Get into the habit of challenging your thoughts, especially if you believe them. *Challenge your thoughts and beliefs by asking if the thoughts or beliefs are true.* If they are not true, do not believe them. Believe only the Truth.

If you do not know the truth concerning a specific thought or belief, work at finding the truth. Acknowledge you do not know the truth at the present time regarding a certain thought. *Do not believe the thought until you discern the truth.* For example, if you believe someone does not like you, to find the truth, ask the person whether or not your perception is true. Simply ask the person if they like you or not. A second example, at a much deeper level of awareness, would be discovering you believe "I am of no worth". You do not have to believe this belief. Do not believe this belief no matter how engrained it may be. The Truth is "You are of worth". "You are precious". "You are important". "You do exist". This level of thought awareness is closely linked with the awareness of feelings.

Acknowledge untrue, hateful, rejecting, condemning, negating, criticizing and judgmental thoughts once you identify them. Stand back and observe these thoughts. Observe the intensity of these thoughts. Express these thoughts in a safe environment without hurting yourself or anyone else. Express the thoughts out loud. As you become fully aware of these thoughts, gently shift your attention to deeper within and work at becoming aware of the emotions and deep beliefs driving these thoughts. What do you feel? What do you sense within?

Use these types of thoughts as indicators of unprocessed inner wounds and lack of connection to Being.

Work at connecting to Being. Thoughts are often fuelled by unconscious painful inner wounds. The mind tries to rationalize these painful inner wounds by thinking and projecting all kinds of false thoughts and false judgments towards yourself and others. Become aware. Ask yourself..."What is the Truth?" Believe only the Truth no matter what your thoughts or feelings tell you. Seek the Truth in all things.

If you discover thoughts that are hateful toward yourself, reject yourself, condemn yourself, negate yourself, judge yourself, put yourself down or criticize yourself, be aware that this is how you have been taught to treat yourself. Each one of these thoughts will have a specific emotion and inner sensation associated with it. You do not deserve to be hated, rejected, condemned, negated, judged, put down or criticized. You never deserved to be treated this way, especially as a child. You deserved and deserve to be accepted, wanted, seen, heard, understood, respected, recognized, validated, cared for, protected and loved. You deserve loving attention. You deserve hearing the Truth of who you Are. You are of great Worth. You are Good. You are a Person. You Exist. You Are. You are Love. You deserve to be Loved.

Begin loving yourself by recognizing thoughts of self hate, self judgment, self rejection, self condemnation, self negation and self criticism. Become aware of these thoughts. Acknowledge these thoughts. Accept that you think these thoughts. Say no to these ways of relating to yourself. Just recognizing these types of thoughts starts to dissolve their power. Begin to accept, want, hear, see, understand and believe yourself. Learn to love yourself. Be gentle with yourself. Give yourself attention. Be present to yourself. Be kind to yourself. Be present to your emotions and inner sensations. This is what you need and deserve. This is what you have always needed and deserved. Be patient and persevere. It takes time to change hurtful engrained ways of relating to yourself. Recognizing these hurtful types of thoughts is closely connected to awareness of emotions and inner sensations.

In summary, thought awareness requires gentle attentiveness, in the present moment, to your thoughts with no judgment. Start by asking yourself *"what am I thinking right now?"* Identifying thoughts is the beginning of inner awareness. It is a simple yet important skill and worth remembering and using.

CHAPTER FIVE

Awareness of Emotions
And Inner Sensations

Get used to your feelings no matter how uncomfortable
they are. Become friends with your feelings. Feelings
will not kill you. Feelings will come but will also go.

Experiencing intense feelings does not mean you are going crazy. Intense feelings can make it "seem" like you are going crazy. You are not! Denying feelings leads to "acting out" of feelings. Feelings can be blind guides in choosing your behavior and actions.

Awareness of feelings takes a bit more time and patience although it is still quite simple to get started. It requires the skills already learned in thought awareness. Awareness of feelings is very exciting. It is a huge step in getting to *know* yourself.

The word "feelings" needs to be defined to prevent confusion and provide clarity. "Feelings" is a word used to refer to *emotions and inner sensations* but it is also a word used to refer to the *capacity to feel*.

The capacity to feel is a sacred part of the human person and is linked to Being.

When referring to the capacity to feel, the word feelings is used interchangeably with the word sensibility. The word feelings or the word sensibility refers to the part of the person that contains and transmits emotions and inner sensations in the body. Feelings or the sensibility may be part of the body's nervous system. The sensibility is located throughout the body. Emotions and inner sensations vibrate in the sensibility, that is, vibrate in the body. Emotions and inner sensations are felt in the body. The mind can become aware of and connected to these emotions and inner sensations in the body.

Feelings = Emotions and Inner Sensations
also,
Feelings = The capacity to feel. = Sensibility

The human being's capacity to sense emotions in the body is due to two important components. Emotions are distinct vibrations or sensations in the body. This is the first component. For example fear, anger, sadness or anxiety are vibrations or sensations felt in the body. Many people are not aware emotions are felt in the body. In fact, the vibrations or sensations associated with deep emotions can be confused with sensations caused by physical body pain. Some deep emotions are felt as intense pain in the body. This type of pain is not caused by a physical ailment. This type of pain is an inner reaction to a life experience, destructive inner mechanisms and believed core lies.

The second component is the mind's ability to "sense" the vibrations of emotions in the body. The combination of these two components enables sensing of emotions and inner sensations. This capacity to sense emotions could be thought of as a "sixth sense". Emotions and inner sensations are the vibrations felt or sensed in the body. The mind can sense and become aware of these vibrations if it is silently attentive.

Emotions and inner sensations occur because you are alive. These vibrations are inner reactions to conscious and unconscious thoughts, beliefs, attitudes, perceptions, wounds, life events and life experiences. Feelings are uniquely personal inner expressions in response to life experiences. Feelings are an inner vibration or an inner type of energy. To dissipate, feelings need to be felt and expressed through the body. If feelings are not felt and expressed, they are stored in the body. As a result, these unprocessed or unfelt feelings can create a pathway to your unconscious, especially when these same unprocessed feelings are awakened by present day triggers. These stored emotions and inner sensations create opportunities for the revelation of unconscious thoughts, beliefs, attitudes, inner mechanisms, traumas and inner pain from past unprocessed life experiences. You hold your reactions to these unprocessed experiences deep inside. In this regard your feelings are the voice for all the repressed reactions to life experiences which have been stored in your psyche. The psyche is made up of the mind, sensibility and body.

Your present day emotions and inner sensations are a key to healing mental, emotional and spiritual wounds from the past and the present.

These wounds are associated with inner pain. Inner pain can be conscious or what is very often the case, can be deeply buried in the unconscious and even buried so deeply as to the point of being concretized.

Your feelings let you know much about yourself, most importantly, all about what the mind is not aware of or has forgotten. Your feelings, or more specifically your emotions and inner sensations, can begin to lead you to "in-depth" consciousness. Your task is to learn to identify emotions and inner sensations. Work at becoming aware of your emotions and inner sensations. Become attentive to your feelings. Become present to your feelings.

Learning to sense your feelings is the first step. Sensing feelings begins by simply becoming aware you feel "something" within. At this stage you do not need to be aware what the feeling is. The feeling can be vague and ill defined. You just become aware of the inner sensation.

This "something" you feel may be just a single emotion or could be a group of complex emotions.

As with awareness of thoughts, learning to sense feelings begins by becoming *silent* and *still*. Take a deep breath or two and become present. Be here in the now. Let go of the past and the future. Think of your attention, that is your attentiveness, as a flashlight. Shine your flashlight of attention on some external object a few feet away. Just be attentive to the object for a few moments. Now bring your attention to your body by looking at your index finger. Be attentive to your index finger. Just look at your finger without thinking about anything else. Now rub your thumb and your index finger together and close your eyes. Bring your total attention to what you feel when you rub your index finger and thumb together. In stillness and silence with your eyes remaining closed, continue to be attentive to what this feels like. As you stop rubbing your fingers together remain still, both outside and inside. Shift your attention from your fingers to your whole body. Shift your attention to "within" your body.

Focus your attention within your body to the areas of your forehead, jaw, tongue, neck, shoulders, chest, back, abdomen, arms and legs. Be *still* in silence as you shine attentiveness within your body. Let your mind be still. Suspend thoughts or thinking. Do not try to do anything. Do not try to be aware of anything. Just be attentive and open to *within* with no demand, expectation or judgment of yourself or what you feel or do not feel. Just hang out here for a moment. Do you sense anything in the area within your chest, back or abdomen? Do you sense anything within your head, neck or limbs? Do not try to name or "figure out" anything...just observe. "Be with" whatever you observe. If you feel or sense anything, "welcome" this part of you. Be accepting of what you sense or feel. Be accepting of what you discover. Be calm, gentle, non judgmental, accepting and at peace even if you think you have not experienced anything. After a few moments take a couple of deep breaths, become aware of your surroundings and open your eyes. In time you will begin to sense the vibrations of your emotions and inner sensations in your body.

Learning to identify specific emotions is the second step. Specific emotions are emotions like anger, fear or sadness. Learning how to hear what your feelings say or reveal is the very exciting and life giving third step. This third step is the process of putting words to the content of emotions and inner sensations.

To approach your feelings, the most important attitude to convert to is one of **no judgment**...just Gentleness, Openness, Honesty, Transparency, Acceptance, Patience and Humility. Humility is not humiliation. Humility is the non-judgmental awareness, acknowledgement and acceptance of **what is**. What is...Is. No judgment. Let go of the internal fight to judge, negate, reject, hate, ignore or repress your emotions or yourself for having the emotions. Receive your emotions. Recognize your emotions. Pay attention to your emotions. Allow your emotions. Allow your feelings. Be gentle with your feelings.

Your feelings are sacred. Your feelings have much to reveal to you.

Your feelings are "your" inner reactions. Welcome your feelings. Do not "act out" of your feelings. Do not hurt yourself, others or your environment. Your feelings do not define who you Are. Your feelings can be a symptom of abuse, hurt, trauma and lovelessness that you have experienced in your life. Your feelings can reveal core lies and self destructive inner mechanisms. Your feelings can lead you to pockets of unprocessed inner pain. Remember, there is much more to you than your feelings.

Moments of awareness of thoughts, emotions, inner sensations or Being are marked by an "inner shift".

An inner shift is sensed as more inner peace, a lightness, inner space, inner clarity, inner harmony, a sense of oneness, connectedness, inner expansiveness, an understanding of self and/or as an "ah hah" moment...an **awe** moment. This experience can be very slight or quite marked. As pertaining to feelings, an inner shift is a time when the intellect identifies, understands or hears the inner vibrations or emotions sensed and felt in the body. A shift occurs when you put words that correspond to an emotion or inner sensation.

Awareness marked by an inner shift can be as simple as realizing that you experience or feel "something" within. The next step is to realize that the something is an emotion or a group of emotions. It is very easy to jump over, ignore, deny or miss emotions and inner sensations; especially if these feelings have been suppressed or repressed throughout much of your life.

For now, learn to put a name to your emotions without doing anything about them. Learn to identify, acknowledge and accept your emotions. Become comfortable with your emotions. **Be with** your emotions. You may need to begin by acknowledging and accepting that you sense nothing within. This is a common experience after a lifetime of steeling yourself to your emotions. Steeling yourself to your emotions can be a result of abuse, lovelessness or other major trauma. You may need to begin by acknowledging that you hate your emotions, or that you do not like or want your emotions. If this is the case, quite simply for now just accept that you cannot accept "what is" or you do not want to accept what is...with no judgment. In the meantime work at nurturing your awareness of and connection to Being. Learn that Gentleness and Acceptance is within you. Replace self judgment with Gentleness, Acceptance and Connection. You Are. You Exist.

Acknowledging emotions is life-giving and an act of existence. Acknowledging emotions will not kill you or make you a lesser person. Imagine an innocent and vulnerable child with the emotions you experience. How would you treat this child? This can help awaken the love, compassion, gentleness, caring, understanding, kindness, patience, acceptance and tenderness within you and help you turn away from self judgment, self rejection, self condemnation and self hate. You need and deserve the same love, recognition, acceptance and attention you would give a child.

The "awareness" of an emotion will progress to "identifying" the emotion. Many people are not able to identify the emotions they experience. Begin learning the skill of emotional awareness by identifying and owning simple emotions such as anger, fear, hate, anxiousness, sadness, hurt, guilt, grief, frustration, disappointment, loneliness, pain, shame, jealousy or sorrow. Identify common feelings such as feeling overwhelmed or confused. Then, identify more complex feelings such as the feeling that life is difficult. Put a name or phrase to what you feel inside...with gentleness and with no judgment. Experiment with different words to name an emotion or inner sensation.

You will experience an inner shift when the words match the emotion or inner sensation you experience within.

To learn to put words to your feelings, a helpful exercise is to think of an upset child standing in front of you. You are attentive and present to the child. You want to hear and receive the child's pain. You want to connect to the child. If the child is afraid, angry or crying; what do you want from the child? You want to understand the child's pain. For this to happen the child needs to express in words what he or she is feeling and experiencing. You want to know why the child is feeling this way. Is the child feeling unloved, left out, not important, not wanted, rejected, judged, abandoned or condemned? Is the child afraid of being hurt?

To heal inner pain, you must become as a child. You need to not only become aware of your emotions and inner sensations, you must also feel and express them. Express your pain as freely, innocently and authentically as a child expresses his or her pain. Do this with yourself at first. In time, hopefully you can find someone you trust who is loving, present, faithful and non judgmental to receive your pain. Expressing your pain to someone who is a loving Presence speeds healing and is deeply healing. Love, Life and Presence touch the Love, Life, Presence and Truth within You.

With this in mind be still and be attentive within. Give your total attention and presence to You---to what you sense within. What emotions do you sense? Are you feeling sad? Are you feeling hurt or afraid? If so, can you put words to the fear or the pain? Do you feel like you are not good enough, no good, not important, worthless, or nothing. Do you feel unloved, not wanted, not accepted, not seen, not understood, not respected, rejected, judged, condemned, hated, shamed, negated, ridiculed or criticized? This exercise may help you on the road to identifying your emotions and inner sensations. You identify your emotions and inner sensations by putting words to them.

As briefly mentioned, many people feel blank or numb inside and may not be aware they feel any emotions. This is in itself part of identifying emotions. Feeling numb is an emotion. Some people feel depressed or flat. Your emotions are just below these superficial sensations. If this is the case, start by becoming aware of the times you experience anger. Almost everyone feels anger. For people who are not connected to their feelings, anger is quite often very intense and frequent. Anger is often covered or hidden by depression. Depression can be a result of suppressing anger.

Be attentive to any other emotions you may experience. Practice being attentive to your emotions; that is, be attentive within. What do you sense within? Be on the lookout for any emotions you may be overlooking. Be patient and gentle with yourself.

People often deny their anger because this emotion is erroneously judged as negative, bad, dangerous and wrong. Furthermore, people wrongly conclude, if the emotion of anger is bad and if they are angry, then *they* are bad. People are wrongly judged as bad, no good, negative, crazy, out of control, dangerous and/or wrong if they feel anger. Your emotions are never bad, wrong or negative. Emotions just are. "You" are not bad, no good, wrong, a failure or weak for having emotions; no matter what the emotions are. You as a human being are never a mistake, wrong, bad, no good or unacceptable. "Acting out" of an emotion in a violent, abusive or destructive way towards self, another person or someone's property is the part that is wrong or bad and often very dangerous. As previously discussed, the *behavior* is what can be seen as wrong, bad, negative and no good...not the emotion and not you. Separate the behavior from the person. Separate your behavior from You.

Acting out of an emotion occurs when emotions are unconscious. Emotions become unconscious when denied, ignored, hidden, stuffed, suppressed and repressed. Acting out of an emotion occurs when emotions are not acknowledged and safely felt and expressed. Emotions are repressed and not acknowledged because of fear of rejection, hate, wrath, condemnation, negation, abuse, punishment, shame, guilt and judgment.

An emotion can be felt, received and expressed without "acting out" of the emotion. Anger can be expressed in a constructive, safe and healing way. The raw expression of anger can be violent in the sense that the expression of the anger is very intense at times. But this violent expression does not mean hurting yourself, others or property. The healthy violent expression of anger is not violence "acted out" against self, others or someone's property. You can "feel" anger and rage but do not hurt yourself, others or property. For example, you can feel and express anger and rage by yelling, screaming, growling or by hitting or kicking a pillow or punching bag. There are many ways to express anger through the body which are not hurtful or abusive. This expression of the felt anger is done in a safe environment alone or with a safe and trusted person such as a good friend or therapist. Beneath intense anger is inner pain caused by past hurts, core lies and lovelessness.

Do not use this expression of anger to frighten or intimidate others. It is very tempting to want to attack others instead of focusing within and "feeling" your anger and pain. It is very tempting to shift your attention from your emotions within and focus your attention to that which is external. By external I mean the present day persons, events or situations on the outside of you.

It can seem so very real that the person in front of you in the present day is responsible for your anger, fear and pain.

Frightening, intimidating, oppressing or manipulating people with your anger is not a healing expression of anger. These behaviours are the result of the unconscious blaming of others for your pain or wanting to protect yourself from facing core lies and inner pain. With that being said, it is very healing to have someone "receive" your anger. This is much different than trying to frighten or intimidate someone with your anger. When someone receives your anger this person is paying attention to you with love. This person is present to you. This person is present to you, present to your expression of anger and present to your pain. There are present day people and situations which can be hurtful, in which case a "proportionate" response of anger is appropriate. These are fine lines. Mistakes will happen in the beginning of emotional awareness work. It is very helpful to find someone who has been on this journey and is aware of the process of healing, to guide you through these difficult times when deep and intensely painful emotions begin to surface.

Inner wounds resulting from lovelessness are felt in the body.

Inner wounds are initially sensed "within" as a vague group of emotions. This group of emotions is an example of an inner sensation. The emotions and pain from inner wounds can feel like a pressure, burning, tightness, aching, tenseness, spasm or pain in the body. Initially inner wounds can be experienced as a sense of numbness, flatness, darkness, emptiness, blackness, nothingness or as a sense of feeling dead within. Do not be afraid. This is the beginning of healing the inner wounds, which cause these inner sensations. These inner sensations need to be explored, understood and expressed. "Be with" these feelings. Become comfortable with the uncomfortable. You are much more than these wounds and feelings.

With practice, emotional awareness progresses to "in-depth" emotional awareness. In-depth emotional awareness is the ability to identify the "content" of deep emotions and inner sensations. Identifying the content of deep emotions and inner sensations is the process of putting specific words to these emotions and inner sensations. Putting words to deep emotions and inner sensations leads to awareness of unprocessed inner pain, awareness of destructive inner mechanisms and awareness of unconscious core lies you believe about self, others and God.

Further, in-depth emotional awareness is the process of receiving and expressing deep emotions and inner sensations through the body. In-depth emotional awareness is an important step in the process of healing inner wounds. Inner wounds are caused by lovelessness, loss and other traumatic life experiences. If your feelings reveal to you ways of relating to yourself that include self hate, self rejection, self condemnation, self judgment, or self negation—know that these feelings have been inflicted by the ways of lovelessness. You have been taught these ways of relating to yourself. Be patient, as these inner relational patterns with self are most likely deeply engrained. It will take awareness of these hurtful inner mechanisms to dismantle them. Awareness comes from being gently attentive to your feelings. Further, you must connect to your Being, that is your Love, Life, Presence and Truth to learn a new way of relating to yourself. This new way is based in Love and Truth which is the essence and core of who you Are. Love and Truth is the foundation of Life...the way of Life.

Remember do not act out of your emotions in an abusive, hurtful, damaging or self destructive way. Do not hurt yourself. Do not hurt others. Be patient and persevere. You need to balance this work of awareness. You need time to forget about the work of awareness. Just leave it for awhile. Go for a walk, have a game of golf, go out with friends, go into nature, go to work or go to a movie. Live your life.

CHAPTER SIX

Awareness of the Body

The body is not only the temple of the mind and emotions, but also the Spirit. Your body manifests your Spirit in this physical plane of existence. It is important to take time to be aware of the body. The body is physical and as such has limits. The mind, emotions and Spirit need to function within the limits of the body.

The body transmits and reveals physical sensations related to intimacy, hunger, physical pain, warmth, coldness, tiredness, nutritional needs and the need for exercise. The body enables us to see, hear, touch, smell and taste. Through these senses the Spirit can be touched. Within the body is contained the capacity to feel, that is the capacity to experience emotions and inner sensations. Within the body is the capacity to sense the Realities of Being. Within the body is the intellect's path to Being. The body is the sacred and precious temple of your Spirit.

The body holds much wisdom. The body alerts you to physical, emotional and spiritual needs. The body holds a record of what you have experienced in your life. The body holds your inner reactions to life experiences associated with unprocessed feelings and experiences. Unprocessed inner pain as well as unconscious beliefs and attitudes are stored in the body. What the mind forgets, the body remembers. As such your body is a treasure trove of pathways and connections to awareness and healing.

Awareness of physical bodily sensations is closely tied to the awareness of feelings and it can be difficult to discern between the two. The reason for this is that both feelings and physical bodily sensations are felt, sensed and experienced in the body. Feelings are emotions and inner sensations. Emotions and inner sensations are felt, processed and expressed through the body. Inner wounds are experienced as emotions and inner sensations in the body. Emotions and inner sensations felt in your body can lead you to awareness of inner wounds.

Your body can lead you to inner wounds buried in the unconscious. By being attentive to your body you can become aware of emotions and inner sensations associated with inner wounds. More specifically, by being attentive to emotions and inner sensations felt in your body, your intellect can be awakened to inner wounds stored in the body. Through loving gentle attentiveness and no judgment, blocks to inner wounds created by the intellect can slowly be weakened and removed. Also, for the blocks to be removed, the intellect must grow in its awareness of and connection to Being. As the blocks are removed, the emotions and inner sensations associated with inner wounds grow in strength and intensity. Now the intellect can stand in the strength of Being and these emotions can be received, acknowledged, accepted, felt and finally expressed through the body.

The intellect can awaken to these inner wounds through any of the body's five senses. Be aware of the inner wounds touched by your senses. Sights, sounds, smells, tastes and touch can trigger inner wounds, as can relationships and life events.

The intellect just stands back and simply allows and observes what is sensed and experienced in the body; whether it involves emotions, inner sensations, needs, pain or movements of your Spirit. At the same time the intellect adopts the attitudes and ways of Attentiveness, Acceptance, Gentleness, Presence and non-judgment. These are the ways of Being...the ways of Love. As the mind adopts these attitudes, it is in fact connecting with Spirit. With time and experience you will be able to discern what you sense in your body.

As with emotions, inner sensations and physical bodily sensations; *Realities of the Spirit are also sensed and felt in the body.* Your mind can be awakened to your Spirit through all the body's senses. Sight, hearing, touch, smell and taste create avenues to your Spirit within. It is within your body that your intellect senses Spirit or Being. The Reality of your Spirit does not depend on your body. Your Spirit Is. Your body is the physical temple of your Spirit. Your body will pass away. Your Spirit will not.

Be aware of what is touched within you through all your senses. Especially be aware of and savour the moments when your Spirit is touched through your senses. These are opportunities to become aware of the Reality and capacities of Being. Be aware when through one or all of your five senses—Awe, Wonder, Beauty, Silence, Stillness,

Kindness, Caring, Clarity, Presence, Warmth, Acceptance, Gentleness, Goodness, Compassion, Existence, Joy, Peace, Faith and/or Love—are touched. This is within You. This is You. Your body can lead you to your Spirit...to the Reality of Being. The body needs to be taken care of, respected and treated as the precious gift it is.

Your body can lead you to knowing what you think, feel and to what you need physically, mentally, emotionally and spiritually. It is through the body that we relate to, connect and commune with our self, others, nature and our environment. It is through the body that Spirit is lived and expressed. Be attentive to all the parts of your body, to the senses of the body and to all the capacities of the body within the physical, emotional, mental and Spiritual realms.

It is so easy to take the body for granted. Just touch the hair on your forearm. Isn't it amazing how you can feel this touch throughout your whole body? What is your reaction to touch? All aspects of you are connected whether or not you are aware. Take time to be silent to listen to your body and to enjoy and appreciate all its wonders, mystery and wisdom.

CHAPTER SEVEN

Awareness of Spirit or Being

During the most difficult times of my illness when the suffering was too much to bear, I developed an instinctual reflex. Without realizing what I was doing, I would become silent and still and I would inwardly sink down deep into the depths of who I am. Here there was peace. Here there was a relief. Here there was solidity. Here I was protected from the storm raging above me, around me and within me. Here I was safe from the fires of hell even though it felt like I was walking through the flames. I didn't know it at the time but I was sinking into the depths of my Being. There was nowhere else to go. There was nothing else I could do. I was imprisoned by the illness. I had never before known this power and yet when I think about it I unconsciously had the deep inner sense that it was always there.

The awareness of Being is a deep inner experience. Awareness of Being is a sense of Amness, Presence, Peace, Acceptance, Joy, Oneness,

Awe, Wonder, Connection, Life, Gratitude, Harmony, Strength, Love and more. The awareness of Being is the intellect awakening to Being. The intellect realizes Being. The intellect connects to Being. The deepest awareness of Being is the inner sense of the Presence of the Creator.

In the deepest part of your Being is the Presence of the

Creator. In the deepest part of your Being is

communion with the Creator.

It is difficult to convey this Reality.

Awareness of Spirit or Being is the bedrock foundation to the work of personal growth and healing. Awareness of Spirit is at the same time the awareness of Existence. Awareness of Existence is the awareness "I Am".

Spirit is who you really Are. Spirit is the depths of you. Spirit or Being is your rock. Language takes away from the power and Reality of Spirit...of Being. Words are inadequate and fail to communicate this Reality. You need to "see" for yourself. You need to live this Reality. You need to connect to Being. You enter into Being, that is, into the depths of who you Are, through awareness. Silence, stillness and attentiveness "within" lead to awareness.

With the awareness of Being comes the awareness of Reality and Truth, the awareness of Existence and also the awareness of Be-ing.

Being is the deeper Reality. Being is Reality. Be-ing is the act of "existing" in who you Are. Be-ing is living who you Are.

To prevent confusion and provide clarity it is important to note the word Being has different but closely connected meanings. Being can be used to refer to the Spirit, the Essence or the Center of a person. The Spirit or Core of a person is the very depths of the person. It is the awareness of Being that makes you feel at home in your skin. You no longer need to prove or justify yourself. At the very depths of a person is Love, Truth, Life, Peace, Acceptance, Presence, Existence, Amness, Connection, Goodness, Joy, Determination, Awe, Wonder, Gentleness, Caring, Patience, Silence, Stillness, Sorrow, Long suffering, Kindness, Oneness, Communion, Strength, Enthusiasm...and these Realities are never ending.

Being also refers to Existence. Awareness of Existence is the awareness of "I Am". The awareness "I Am" has a sense of solidity in the knowing that "I exist". Spirit/Being is the source of Existence. In fact, Spirit or Being is Existence. All else will pass. The awareness "I Am" is the awareness of Being. The awareness "I Am" is connection to Being. In that awareness and connection to what is real...to what is Reality...is the solid sense "I exist"...that is, the solid sacred sense..."I Am".

Finally, *Be-ing refers to existing in who you Are.* Making choices, having an opinion, having a voice, saying what you need to say, saying no to lies, taking your space, consciously choosing to believe Truth, expressing and living your Truth, living your Life and expressing your Love are examples of existing in who you Are. "Being" is your Love, Life, Existence, Presence and Truth. "Be-ing" is to Be who you Are. Being is living who you Are. Be-ing is living from your Spirit, that is, living from who you Are while accepting and living all of you. Be-ing brings you into relationship with yourself, others and your Creator.

Acceptance of all of you comes from Spirit. A simple example of this mystery of Spirit within all of us is the realization that...I can accept that "I cannot accept" or I can accept that for now "I do not want to accept". Just this simple inner awareness and "shift" brings Peace, Life and Harmony within. In Being you cannot lose. Peace and Harmony replace the unconscious inner fighting with self.

You can Be in good times and you can Be in difficult times. You can Be through great pain. You can Be with tumultuous emotions and inner sensations. You can Be with your emotional, intellectual and physical limitations. This is the Strength, Solidity and Reality of Being which is often missed. Being is the awareness of "Amness". Ultimately your Being—that is, your Love, Life, Existence, Presence and Truth— is who you Are.

Your Love, Life, Existence, Presence and
Truth are enough.

Uncomfortable raging emotions do not negate Being. Feeling numb, dead or empty within does not negate Being. Illness and physical pain do not negate Being. Deeply engrained untrue thoughts, beliefs and attitudes, which are often unconscious, do not negate Being. Core lies do not negate Being. Believing core lies does not negate your Being. Inner pain does not negate Being. Lack of awareness of Being does not negate Being. All of the above "feel" like they negate Being. They do not. Your Being or Spirit is within; whether you know it or not, want it or not, or feel it or not. Being is deeper than the turmoil. It is because of Being you are able to survive the turmoil. Your Spirit does not depend on whether or not you are conscious. Your work is to become aware of and reconnect to the priceless gift of your Spirit and Life within.

Reconnect to the Reality of Being.
This is what it means to be conscious.

Spirit or Being is who you Are and no one or no thing or no power can destroy Spirit or take your Spirit from you. Spirit is home. Spirit always Is. We search and long for Spirit or Being. The search can take our whole life. Sadly even after a lifetime, awareness of Spirit can evade us, but this does not negate Spirit. Do not be afraid. Be silent and still within. Spirit is You...whether you are aware or not.

Spirit or Being is the answer to the emptiness felt within. Spirit is as real as any part of the physical body. Spirit is so very gentle. Spirit demands and expects nothing. This is your deepest Reality. Spirit just Is. Spirit is Reality. This is a statement the intellect or mind can have great difficulty accepting and for this reason "awareness" of Spirit/Being is a precious gift beyond worth. The mind or intellect will come to see Reality. The intellect needs to let go of the automatic and programmed self judgment, self hate, self condemnation, self rejection and self negation and both connect to Being and adopt the ways of Being as a new way of relating to self and others.

Words are limited when attempting to describe Being, and yet they are a necessary beginning. There are no words to really describe Being or Spirit. Words are a means of communication with the mind or intellect. Words can lead us or point us to experience Being. Words of Truth can create connection to Being. Experiencing Being goes beyond words, thoughts and feelings. Experiencing Being is coming to "know" for yourself who you Are. Being is not a fantasy or imagining. Being is real. Spirit or Being is your Center. Experiencing Being is entering into Being.

Awareness of Being takes us deeper than feelings. We can mistake the sensing of Being as emotions or feelings. We can wrongly conclude that the consciousness of Being is an emotion or feeling. Being is not an emotion or feeling. For example, the sensing of Peace within can be falsely thought of as a peaceful "feeling". Peace is from your Being. It is solid and much deeper than emotions. This is why you can be at Peace even through intense emotions or difficult situations. It is from the solidity of Being you are able to experience intense and seemingly overwhelming emotions and situations.

This confusion between emotions and Realities of Being happens because the brain or intellect receives the sense of emotions from the sensibility, but also receives the sense of Spirit Realities from the sensibility. Emotions vibrate in the sensibility. The sensibility is the part of the body that contains and vibrates emotions. The intellect can sense the vibrations of emotions in the sensibility. The sensibility enables the capacity to feel and to sense emotions. Biologically, the sensibility may be a part of the body's nervous system, but the sensibility is also probably a part of the Spirit or an extension of the Spirit. At any rate, the sensibility is linked or connected to the Spirit. As mentioned in a previous chapter, the sensibility and the brain's ability to detect vibrations in the sensibility may be thought of as a sixth sense. The sensibility is a means by which the body, mind, emotions and Spirit are connected. The sensibility is a means by which the body, mind, emotions and Spirit communicate with each other. The sensibility is contained within the entire body.

The sensibility vibrates or transmits emotions; however, the sensibility is also illuminated by the Spirit.

The intellect senses both the emotional vibrations and Spirit Realities in the sensibility. However, if you are very silent and still in the present moment and very gently attentive, you may sense the depth, solidity and vastness of your Spirit. The Spirit illuminates the sensibility but is "not" an emotion originating in the sensibility. The Spirit is much deeper than emotions. The Spirit is the core and foundation of who you Are. Spirit is who you Are. Spirit or Being is Reality. The Spirit not only illuminates the sensibility, but also the mind and the body. The Spirit illuminating the sensibility, mind and body enables Be-ing.

To simplify this subject it is necessary only to remember that emotions and inner sensations are sensed and felt in the body. Emotions and inner sensations vibrate in the body. Emotions associated with inner wounds originate in the sensibility part of the body. Realities of Being originate from the Spirit. Realities of Being illuminate the sensibility, mind and body.

Inner wounds block the intellect's awareness of and connection to Being. Inner wounds are composed of core lies and inner pain. The inner pain comes from a variety of sources. Inner wounds can block Being and Be-ing. Inner healing removes blocks to Being. Awareness of thoughts, emotions, inner sensations, body and Spirit enables inner healing.

To understand this aspect of healing, think of your Spirit as a bright light. Now imagine covering up the light with stones or chunks of mud. The light is blocked by the stones and mud. The light is your Being or Spirit. The stones and chunks of mud are inner wounds. The light is not extinguished by the stones and mud, only blocked.

As the blocks are removed, the mind
begins to see the light.

Healing inner wounds by growing in awareness of and connection to mind, emotions, inner sensations, body and Being removes these blocks. Inner clarity results from awareness. Inner clarity is a process. Inner clarity happens when the mind connects to thoughts, emotions, inner sensations, body and Spirit. Inner clarity occurs when the mind becomes aware of and connects to the Truth and Reality of Being.

Healing inner wounds removes the intense distractions and dark voids of inner pain, core lies, self destructive inner mechanisms and lack of connection to Being.

That is to say, when the inner pain of lovelessness is felt and expressed; when core lies such as "I am worthless", "I am no good", "I am nothing", "I am not important" and/or "I am not" are identified; when self rejection, self judgment, self condemnation, self hate and self negation are recognized and when the light of Love, Life, Presence, Existence and Truth is experienced within, life can be lived to the full. The stones and chunks of mud are cleared away. The light of Being can now radiate through the mind, body and emotions.

Inner clarity persists and increases as inner wounds are healed. As inner wounds are healed their intense vibrations in the sensibility are decreased. Healing inner wounds clears the intellect's path to Being.

Even through the deepest, darkest and most pervasive inner wounds; pinpoint rays of light from Being shine forth. Being cannot be denied by any power; not even lovelessness. These pinpoint rays of light are moments of connection to Being. The intellect connects to Being. Nurture these moments of awareness of and connection to Being. Decide and choose to take time to nurture these moments of awareness and connection.

Stillness and silence can open the intellect to awareness of Being. The intellect needs only to be gently attentive in the present moment to what Is...without demand, expectation or judgment. This sounds simple, but "simple" does not necessarily mean easy. Inner wounds block awareness of Being and fuel infinite numbers of distractions, imaginings, behaviours and defenses. Be patient and persevere. Spirit is gentle but profoundly powerful. In gentleness, let go of self judgment. Also, let go of demands and expectations of yourself. Take time to nurture awareness of Being. Choose to take time to Be.

Practice being still and silent each day. In the stillness and silence be attentive to the deep Reality within. Let your thoughts come and go. Let your feelings or emotions be. Allow your body all its aches, pains and sensations. Acknowledge your thoughts, feelings and body. Be with your thoughts, emotions and body. Put to the side all external distractions and situations. Become aware of the present moment. Turn away from the past and the future. Let go of what has happened in the past and what will happen in the future. The present moment is all you have. Now in silence and stillness shift your attentiveness deeper within. Have no expectation of yourself. Make no demands of yourself. Close your eyes. Slowly and gently take three to four deep breaths. Slowly breathe in deeply through your nose and then out through your nose or mouth. Be gentle. Drop into the depths of who you Are. Can you sense a Silence and Stillness within...can you sense a Peace and Solidity within...can you sense a Presence within...or can you sense Love, Oneness, Awe, Gratitude, Gentleness, Connection, Acceptance, Life, Sacredness, Communion or Harmony within? This is Your Spirit.

This is Your Being. Just a glimpse...just a moment of awareness is powerful and can change your life forever.

Take deep breaths while you stand back and observe your thoughts, feelings and body with gentle acceptance and without judgment. As you take deep breaths you will automatically be drawn deeper into yourself. This deeper part of yourself is your Spirit. At the same time you may feel fear, anger or other emotions. Be with these emotions but gently shift your attentiveness to the deeper Solidity within. This deeper part of yourself is your Presence. This deeper part is the Peace and Solidity that is You. This is You. This is who you really Are. Enter into this Peace, Acceptance and Presence. Do not try to grab it or control it. This is the ego part of your intellect trying to possess it. Just let this tendency go. Go back to observing and acceptance. It is all okay. You are okay. You Are.

The act of standing back and becoming the observer of your thoughts, body and especially your emotions is an exercise of entering into Being. From Being you are able to watch your emotions. From Being you can allow your emotions to be, without acting out of them. From Being you can **accept** and **Be** with your emotions. From Being you can observe your thoughts and emotions without judgment. In Being there is Harmony, Acceptance, Oneness, Communion and Peace.

"Being" does not take away "all" uncomfortable feelings or life's challenges and difficulties. The strength and solidity of Spirit...of Being, enables you to BE with all...to Be with all your thoughts, feelings, body and life experiences. Being enables you to go through all. Spirit allows us to Be. We can Be with our self and we can Be with others. We can speak our truth and act out of our Love and Truth. The power of Being heals inner wounds and the associated inner pain from believed core lies, non-existence, loss and lovelessness. Awareness of Being is awareness of Truth. Become aware of Truth and Being to heal core lies and wounds so you can live your Life to the full.

Meditation, life-touching people, journaling, nature, time in nature, time alone to Be, life-touching work, exercise, life's mission, trials, tribulations, passions, silence, stillness, spiritual traditions and exercises, times of closeness with your Creator, acts of kindness and life-touching books, music, movies and art are among the many ways to touch and awaken capacities of the Spirit to the intellect. Awakening the intellect to capacities of the Spirit creates opportunities for awareness of Being and entering into Being. Allow these moments of Being to permeate your mind, body and emotions. Savour these moments. Take the time to be attentive to these moments. Frequently nurture connection to Being by taking the time to engage in one or more of the above listed paths which lead to awareness of and connection to Being.

Practice Be-ing; that is, bringing Being into relationship.

Presence, Acceptance, Caring, Kindness, Gratitude, Tenderness, Attentiveness, Understanding, Determination, Courage, Strength, Tolerance, Patience, Generosity, Compassion and Love are some of the infinite examples of bringing Being into relationship; that is, into relationship with yourself and with others.

To the mind or intellect, Being would seem not "enough". To the mind or intellect, "Being" may not seem real. On the contrary, Being is the rock of who you Are. More accurately, Spirit or Being is who you Are. Truly blessed are those who can hear this. The experienced awareness of Being is a deep sense of "I Am". The experienced awareness of Being is entering into the deep Peace, Acceptance, Oneness and Presence of who you Are. At the core of Being is Connection, Communion and Oneness with your Creator.

The mind surrenders to this Reality within. There is no longer a need to fight and struggle in an attempt to exist, in an attempt to Be or in an attempt to have others let you Be. You do not have to prove anything to yourself or anyone else. Your Life is within you and always has been. Your Source is within You. Your Life, your Source...that is your Being...does not come from anything or anyone outside you. Your Amness is a given and is within You—is You.

You...Are.   Say... "I Am".

Discussing Being often stimulates the intellect to want it...to want to be able to experience Being. The wants turn into expectations and demands, but just as you might expect or demand to hold water in your hands, the water slips away. So, too, it is with Being. The intellect needs to let go of expectations or demands and just be attentive. The intellect needs to stop trying and stop controlling. Just accept and chuckle when you catch your expectations or demands, then let them go.

Peace is within You. Peace is You.

CHAPTER EIGHT

Meditation

Of all the ways to awaken the intellect to the Reality and Truth of Being, it is my experience that meditation is one of the most powerful. This is not meant to take away from the importance of the many different ways to awaken to Being. All are important. All nurture awareness of Being and connection to Being. There is no "one way" to become aware of and connected to Being.

Living from Being is not a unique or mysterious experience. Living from Being is the way of Life. Many times living from Being is automatic and is not a conscious choice. Living from Being is for everyone. This is how we are created. Problems occur when there are blocks to Being, as is the case with inner wounds. Lovelessness in any one of its many forms can create inner wounds. Further, there are many daily distractions which can pull us out of Being.

Meditation brings us back to our center. Meditation brings us back to and realigns us with Spirit. Meditation grounds the intellect in Reality. Meditation grounds the intellect in Being. Meditation in a simple and yet profound way, paves a path through the infinite distractions associated with thoughts, emotions, the body, untrue beliefs, core lies and inner pain. The path leads to the bedrock of who we Are. *Meditation creates a path connecting the intellect to Being and then, even further, to the center of Being where there is connection and communion with the Creator.* There is such sacredness in every human Being.

There are many types of meditation, but there is one specific type I use in my own practice. Actually, it's not so much a type of meditation but rather, a way of meditation. The meditation I am referring to is the meditation taught by John Main.

John Main studied law in Dublin and was a professor of international law at Trinity College. During his career in law he learned the way of meditation. In time he would leave this career and follow a different path. In 1958 he became a Benedictine monk in London. As a monk it was required he give up meditation, but in 1969 he discovered the old teachings of John Cassian and the desert fathers which were at the roots of his own Christian monastic tradition. In these teachings he found the Christian expression of the same meditation he used to practice. In 1975 he opened the first Christian Meditation Center in London. John Main came to Canada in 1977 to establish a new Benedictine monastery and meditation center in Montreal. John Main, O.S.B. died in 1982.

With this being said it is important to clarify that meditation is not a religion, nor does it favor any specific religion. Meditation is a way for all people and for people of all religions. Meditation is not about religious institutions and yet meditation is for all religions.

Meditation is not about trying to be "holy".
Meditation is about becoming "whole".

Meditation is a way to connect the intellect to the heart. Meditation re-links the head to the heart. Meditation is simple. After a few moments practicing meditation however, it becomes quite evident that meditation is not easy. It costs nothing to learn meditation. You need no special equipment. There is no trick to meditation. It is easy to learn. With meditation you have no demands or expectations. In the beginning you need to go in faith; that is, meditate in faith. Meditation makes absolutely no sense to the intellect, especially the ego part of the intellect.

I want to encourage you to begin the practice of meditation if you are not already meditating. Meditation becomes a discipline of the heart. Meditation will lead you to your heart. Meditation clears a path for your intellect to connect to your heart. It is a narrow path. This narrow path leads to Reality. This narrow path leads to the infinity of Being. This path leads to Love and Truth. On this path it seems all is lost and yet all is given. Learn about meditation as taught by the teachings of John Main. Do not become indoctrinated by any teachings on meditation or any teachings on how to meditate. Guard against indoctrination. If you have been wounded by religious teachings or a religious institution, be gentle and patient with yourself. Just learn how to meditate and forget about any associated religious teachings. The purpose of meditation is to reconnect to who you Are in the depths of your Being. Take in only the essence of meditation from any teachings you are exposed to.

Take from teachings about meditation only that which resonates within you.

Leave the rest.

If you are a busy mother or father, needing to care for your children and make a living, use meditation as a time to regenerate. Do not allow meditation to be a burden or just another chore on an endless to-do list. This can be difficult, but I still encourage you to meditate, even if it is only for a minute or two a day. If you are too burdened and exhausted, forget even meditation. Just rest before your Creator. Lie down in the Presence of your Creator and know you are held, wanted, seen, heard and accepted. You have a deep connection with your Creator. You are within your Creator and your Creator is within You.

You are loved as You Are.

Grow in your familiarity with meditation. It is recommended you meditate twenty minutes twice a day, once in the morning and once in the evening. This can seem a daunting task, especially if you work for a living and have others in your care. Times of meditation are not rules set in stone. You will however, see more benefits from meditation if you do it on a daily basis. Meditation times are especially important if you have been wounded, especially if wounded as a child from having experienced lovelessness. If it seems impossible to meditate for twenty minutes twice a day, begin by meditating for a few minutes once a day. Be as faithful as you can to this meditation. *As you sense inner urgings to increase the time of your meditation, be gently faithful to this inner call.* Increase your meditation time from one or two minutes to five minutes and then to ten minutes and so on, until you meditate for twenty minutes once a day. Meditating for twenty minutes once a day is a major accomplishment. You will see the fruits of meditation. The fruits of meditation will motivate you to continue meditating. As time passes and you acquire a certain comfortableness concerning meditation, begin to meditate in the evening following the same process.

For many people meditation can be very difficult. Do not let this discourage you from meditation, especially if you have an inner sense to meditate. Be patient and persevere. It is worth the effort. Grow in meditation in a way that works for you. You may just start with one minute once a day or one minute twice a day. Follow what you sense within you. The important point is to begin.

I will give you a brief description on how to begin to meditate as taught by John Main. This is all you need to get started. If possible however, it is helpful to find others who also meditate. Other people can be a source of support, knowledge and experience. However, companionship is not necessary.

Be aware when searching the internet. There are many distractions which can divert you from the core teachings of meditation. There are many types and variations of meditation. Here is a website (www.johnmain.org) which describes meditation as taught by John Main. It does however, have strong religious overtones. Nevertheless, within the one page is all the information you will need to begin the daily practice of meditation. Disregard the religious overtones if they bother you. Many people have been wounded by religious institutions. John Main is a good man and dedicated his life to spreading the practice of meditation. He saw for himself the value, power and truth of meditation. He is not trying to swindle or convert anyone. When John Main uses the words "Christ within" it is a metaphor for "Love within". In John Main's religious tradition, Christ personified Love. Christ's life and teachings taught and exemplified Love. Christ brought others into relationship at a deeper level, beyond the ways of the world. Christ connected to others and was in communion with others through Love and Presence. Christ connected to the personhood of others...to the Being of others. Christ's communion with others was a Being-to-Being connection. Christ "saw" the person. Sadly, throughout the ages, Christ's message has been lost and twisted. John Main has many tapes which teach, support and encourage the way of meditation. In his voice you will hear a man who has found a precious truth and has devoted his life to spreading this truth.

The World Community of Christian Meditation is an organization that was formed in the footsteps of John Main and keeps his message of meditation alive. It can be accessed through the following website. http://wccm.org

There are also teachings by Fr. Pat Murray which convey the message of meditation. He was a student of John Main and heard the message and truth of meditation at a deep level. After years of being a missionary in Africa, Pat dedicated his life to the message of meditation and personhood. There are a few CDs by Fr. Pat Murray available on the web. To find the CDs do a search for "Fr. Pat Murray" on this website. http://www.eist.ie

The way of meditation is to sit still in silence and say the word. Sit comfortably in an upright position. Do not say the word out loud. Say the word silently and gently within. Meditation is a discipline. It is a discipline in the sense that the mind senses the calling or whispers of the Spirit, gently urging the practice of meditation. Following these urgings, the word is said with absolute abandonment.

The word used in meditation can be any word. The choice of word does not matter. Fr. John Main encouraged the use of the word "Maranatha" which when divided into syllables is Ma-Ra-Na-Tha. The Aramaic word Maranatha means "Come Lord". This is the intellect's petition to the Spirit within.

Simply sit upright and become still and silent. Gently repeat the four syllables over and over from the beginning to the end of meditation. Say the syllables without expectations or demands. Repeat the four syllables for twenty minutes. Put aside and suspend all thoughts, images, ideas, imaginings, ideals, beliefs, judgments, expectations and demands and just say the word. Remain as still as possible. In meditation give your full attention to saying each syllable of the word as you rest in your Spirit. As thoughts or imaginings come into your mind gently let them go and return your complete attention to saying the word. Gently be completely attentive to saying each syllable. Say and listen to each syllable. Say and listen to each ..."Ma"..."Ra"..."Na"..."Tha". In meditation you do not have to "do" anything. Meditation is simple and straight forward. Meditation is a journey. Meditation although simple, is not necessarily easy.

Never judge your meditation or yourself because of the way you meditated. Do not analyze your meditation. The ego wants to analyze, to determine if you are a success or failure or to determine if meditation is a success or failure. Gently turn away from such thoughts and judgments. Let them go. The ego cannot understand meditation. The intellect needs to connect to Being. Every time we meditate, we are all beginners. *What matters is that we begin.* As distractions come, in any of the many forms, simply acknowledge the distraction but then shift your attention to saying the word. Become completely attentive to the word; that is, to each syllable of the word; as you gently repeat the syllables over and over from the beginning to the end of meditation.

Every time you meditate you delete some of the lovelessness programming that was engrained in your mind, body and emotions.

When you say and listen to each syllable of the word, you are deleting some of the lovelessness programming that so much directs your life and damages you living life. Instead of living in anger, rage, hate, resentment, fear, non-existence, self hate, self rejection, self judgment, self condemnation and self negation; you leave all that programming and you give your complete attentiveness to the mantra which takes you deep into the Solidity, Presence, Existence, Life and Love of who you Are. Remember though, when you meditate forget about trying to get some result. You do not have to "do" or "change" anything. You only need to say the syllables of the word and be totally attentive to each syllable. Just say and listen to each syllable from the beginning to the end of your time of meditation. Let go of and turn away from all demands and expectations---even the demand to not have any expectations. It is okay. You are okay.

It is very tempting to despair and "think" you are getting nowhere with meditation. This is a normal reaction. Continue to meditate. In time you will sense "that" which is within. Meditation will lead you to who you Are, and from who you Are, you can live your Life. During meditation saying each "Ma", each "Ra", each "Na" and each "Tha" is a strong act of Existence.

Meditation is a powerful way of coming to know—"I Am".

Such simplicity and yet so powerful, this is the way of meditation. This is the way of saying the word. It is a narrow path. Meditation is complete surrender of the mind before Spirit. In the depths of your Spirit is your Creator. Your body is truly a temple. Deep Peace,

Oneness, Sacredness, Presence, Communion, Connection and Reverence are within You...are You.

CHAPTER NINE

Truth, Untruth and Choice

Without awareness, choice is not possible. There is so much misunderstanding concerning the word "choice". It is important to clarify the meaning of the reality of choice. Today's pop psychology often uses the word choice as a way of trying to control or change another person's behavior by piling up mountains of guilt or shame. "It was your choice; you live with the consequences" is a commonly heard phrase. There is truth in this statement, but when the truth is mixed with mannerisms, body language and voice tones used to judge, condemn, control, demean, punish, oppress, negate or criticize a "person"; the value of this truth turns to malevolence. The truth that "choice often dictates consequences" is subtly and cunningly mixed with the *implied lies* that "the person is bad, no good, a failure, worthless, nothing or that the person should suffer because of his/her choices".

Once untruth is mixed with truth it becomes evil. The

lie is disguised with truth. The untruth

is a wolf in sheep's clothing.

This can result in serious damage. We all have an innate capacity to hear Truth. When we hear Truth we take it in. A Truth, from whatever the source, resonates with the Truth within us which makes it easy to become our belief. If our discernment is not precise, a Truth which has been mixed with a lie can be believed as all Truth. We take it all in as a Truth. It is easy to see the results of evil...of untruth being mixed with Truth. Once a statement containing Truth mixed with untruth is believed, people's behavior is changed. People believing statements of untruth mixed with Truth can attack themselves, others and God. Relationships can be destroyed. People can commit suicide. Families and friends can be torn apart. Violence, greed, deception and abuse can be justified. Great damage can be done to our planet. Society can be in turmoil. Countries can attack and destroy one another. All these things can happen when people believe untruth as Truth. All these things can happen when people believe "lies" as Truth.

Believing lies as Truth happens very easily when lies are "mixed" with the Truth. As just mentioned, mixing a lie with Truth hides the lie. Also, lack of awareness of Spirit, that is, lack of awareness of Being and Truth, creates fertile ground in the psyche for any "lie" to take root. This lack of awareness creates an inner void and opens the mind and emotions to believe lies as Truth, especially when lies are hidden with Truth.

Choice is part of every facet of life. Choice needs to flow from Being. Choice needs to flow from Love, Life and Truth within. Awareness makes choice possible. The most important and fundamental aspect of choice has to do with Self. Not only does choice enable choosing truth concerning everyday topics, but at a much deeper level, choice enables choosing the Truth about self and choosing Being. For this to happen we need to be *conscious.* We need to be *aware.* We need to be aware of Spirit and Truth. We also need to be aware of "what we believe". Further, we need to be aware if "what we believe" is actually a lie or untruth.

Just because we believe something does not make it true.

Also, what we believe is often unconscious, that is, below our level of awareness. Core lies about self are usually unconscious and engrained. We need to become aware of our beliefs. At the same time we need to become aware of the Truth. We need to separate the untruth from the Truth. We need to remove the sheep's clothing to see the wolf. This process provides clarity and enables choice. The Truth nurtures, strengthens, expands, unites and brings freedom.

The Truth will set you free.

The Truth is important at every level of existence, interaction and relationship. Through awareness we come to clearly see "both" the Truth and the untruth. Once we see both the Truth and the untruth we become conscious. Once we are conscious we can make a choice. We can make a conscious choice. A choice based in Truth changes our behavior...changes our life. In other words, to make a conscious choice, it is necessary to be aware—aware of the Truth and aware of the lie. Now you shift from being on automatic to making choices based on awareness and Truth. Do not be surprised how deep in the unconscious lies can hide. Lies are often difficult to see, especially after years of exposure to lovelessness. Your feelings will alert you to unconscious lies if you take the time to listen and become aware. Learn to hear your feelings by putting words to emotions and inner sensations you experience. Putting words to your emotions and inner sensations will lead you to the awareness of unconscious beliefs. Be patient and persevere.

Awareness of Truth is awareness of Spirit or Being. Being is who you Are. Once aware, choices are made for your Life and from your Life. Once conscious, choices are not just white knuckle attempts at change. Awareness of Being, which is entering into Being, dispels and dissolves core lies.

Consciousness enables choosing
Truth instead of untruth.

Consciousness enables choosing Truth instead of evil. In this light, choice is a gift. Choice is powerful. Choice has the power to change. Choice empowers. Choice gives freedom. You can choose once you are aware.

In all things seek the Truth. Especially seek the Truth about yourself. Once you are free from the shackles created by lies, you can experience life to the full. What lies do you believe as truth? What core lies do you believe as truth—about yourself, others and God? What lies mixed with Truth do you believe? Do not panic. Be calm and at Peace. Peace is in You. Awareness is a process. Choosing Truth is an amazing and powerful gift and has nothing to do with guilt, shame, condemnation or judgment. Believing lies about self is the result of experiencing lovelessness and/or abuse.

Choosing Truth with regards to self, frees you to be who you Are. Unearthing the unconscious lies you believe about yourself and at the same time seeing the Truth about yourself brings light into darkness. Everyone has a deep capacity to hear Truth. Trust this capacity. Truth resonates inside. Truth resonates with the Truth within. Truth brings inner peace, lightness, freedom, joy, more inner space and relief. Truth fosters Love for self, others and God.

The mind, body and emotions can resist the Truth. This is the result of lack of awareness of Being and engrained fallacious programming, both of which are caused by having suffered one or many of the numerous forms of lovelessness. Ultimately, lovelessness is the lack of connection and communion, which is especially damaging for the child. Lovelessness creates lack of connection to Self...lack of connection to Being.

Be Patient. Do not judge yourself.

Do not judge where you are at in your journey.

Do not judge, reject, hate, condemn, negate or belittle yourself.

Be gentle with yourself. Accept yourself. Want yourself. Receive

yourself. See yourself. Connect to your Self. You are a Person.

You are Good. You are of great Worth. You Exist. You Are.

A lie is a statement which is not true. A lie is a statement which is false. A belief is something a person accepts as being true or real. Inner lies and core lies are false beliefs which are accepted as truth. The child is especially vulnerable to believing lies and adopting lies as core beliefs and attitudes. The child is especially vulnerable to believing lies as truth if Being is not nurtured and lovelessness is excessive.

Inner lies and core lies are false beliefs which can be learned or believed as truth throughout life. Inner lies and core lies can be engrained and are usually completely unconscious. Core lies are learned from others. Core lies can also be a result of experiencing ominous life events, traumatic life experiences, serious loss, unmet childhood needs for love, abuse and lovelessness. Lovelessness and abuse create inner wounds. Lovelessness and abuse create, instill, teach, engrain, strengthen and propagate unconscious lies about self, others and God.

To become aware of the unconscious lies believed as truth it is necessary to look within. All that you believe is stored in your mind and body. Take time to hear and listen to your emotions.

Present day emotions and inner sensations are key to uncovering "unconscious lies" stored in the mind and body.

The awareness of unconscious beliefs, inner pain and especially the awareness of "who you Are" is not somewhere outside self. The process of awareness happens "within". Having said that; books, nature, spiritual writings, people who are loving and nurturing and the other previously mentioned life-touching resources are very important and valuable aids in awakening the intellect to Love, Life and Truth within. These resources can also bring to consciousness lies believed as truth. It is however, very tempting and attractive to *just* look outside self for answers and avoid looking within. Love, Life and Truth are within. What you believe is also found within. Looking within takes work and commitment. For many, looking within requires learning new skills. The new skills involve learning to be attentive to thoughts, emotions, body and Spirit.

In order to emphasize the following point, it is important to repeat that people, nature and other external resources awaken the intellect to Love, Life and Truth "within". The point to remember is always bring back your attention to what you experience within. Yes, nature is beautiful, peaceful and breathtaking, but it is critically important to realize the Beauty, Peace and Awe that "you" experience from seeing nature are the Realities you have within you. This is the reason you experience them.

When nature takes your breath away, ask yourself,

"What do I sense within me?"

What you sense are inner movements of your Spirit. At these times your intellect is awakening to that which is within You. In other words, your intellect is awakening to Being. You need only slow down to notice and realize the depth of this experience. Become Present. Within you are Beauty, Peace, Stillness, Presence and Awe. You are Beauty, Peace, Stillness, Presence, Awe, Sacredness, Tranquility and Oneness. This is who...You Are. *It is so simple we miss it.* What do life-touching others, nature, music, books, solitude, stillness and silence awaken in You? What do you sense "within"?

Looking outside self for answers is a necessary part of growing and healing. Looking outside self for your Life, for your Being, for your Center, for your Love and Truth is also part of the process of healing, but it is important to realize that the "inner awareness of Being" is the bedrock of healing and reality. Your Life, your Being, your Existence, your Love and Truth do not come from some "one" or some "thing" outside you. Being is within You. Awareness of Being happens within You. Looking outside self for Being—that is, for Love and Truth—is unconscious. Looking outside yourself is important in that it eventually points you home to Being within.

Love, Life, Existence, Presence and Truth from "outside" awaken and nurture the intellect to the Love, Life, Existence, Presence and Truth "within" you.

Looking outside self for Being can be a way of coping with inner pain and inner turmoil. Searching outside Self for Being, that is, for Love and Truth, is an attempt to fill the painful emptiness and void within. It can momentarily relieve the inner pain by distracting you from it. It also relieves the pain by temporarily filling the void caused by abuse, unmet childhood needs for love, unconscious core lies and *the lack of awareness of Truth and Love within.*

Believing lies is painful and causes inner anxiety. Believing lies is often associated with painful inner wounds. Looking outside self can also be an attempt to find answers for this inner pain. When we have no inkling of our Life within, we look outside our self to someone else or something else in a misguided attempt to find the source of our life. As a child, love is the way of Life. At least it is the way life is meant to be. A child needs to be loved, seen, accepted, wanted, heard and recognized. A child needs a Being-to-Being connection. This love nurtures the child's connection to his or her Being. Without this deep and authentic love during childhood, dependency becomes a way of living in adulthood. We search long and hard for that which is already within us—for that to which we needed to be awakened as a child. Awareness leads to connection to Being. Connection to Being heals the wounds caused by lovelessness.

Anything from outside our self is a sign post pointing us home, to within self, to find answers to who we Are. The Truth heard from outside sources will awaken and resonate with the Truth within. Love from outside self awakens the Love within self. Love from others awakens the capacity of Love "within self". It is this inner capacity of Love within self that enables a person to love self. In other words, Love from others awakens the Love within self and thereby "experientially" teaches a person how to Love self from the Love within. Love is a Spirit to Spirit connection and communion. Others can love you, but from this awakening of the Love within, you then need to Love yourself. Shift to the Love awakened within You as the new way of relating to yourself. Turn away from self hate, self judgment, self condemnation, self negation and self rejection as a way of relating to yourself. Let these mechanisms go. Instead, shift to the Love within. Shift to Acceptance, Gentleness, Kindness, Understanding, Patience, Presence, Caring and Compassion. Nurture awareness of and connection to the Love within. Nurture awareness of the Truth within. Connect to the Love and Truth within.

Ultimately what we believe can only be discovered by looking within. It is here you will discover what you believe and be able to discern whether it is Truth or untruth. Outside sources are very important in that they can bring awareness to what you believe within. Outside sources can also point out Truth. This Truth from outside will awaken Truth within. When an external experience affects you, always come back to what is awakened within. Feelings and emotions can be awakened but more importantly your core which is Love, Life, Existence, Presence and Truth can also be awakened. Savour these times when Being is experienced.

It is "within" where you will discover who you Are. Within is where you will find your Life. It is from within that your Spirit, that is, your Love and Truth will be revealed to you. The outside can awaken and resonate with your Life, Love and Truth within.

As discussed, there are four main facets of the human being. These facets are closely interconnected. The four facets are one, yet separate. The four facets are:

1) Mind/Intellect
2) Emotions and the capacity to experience emotion.
3) Body
4) Spirit

Self awareness involves in-depth awareness of all four facets. This in-depth awareness makes choice possible. The corner stone to choosing the Truth is the "experienced" awareness of and connection to the Truth. Awareness of Truth is awareness of Spirit...awareness of Being. Awareness of Truth is found in the awareness of Love. The core or center of a human being is the Spirit which is Love, Life, Presence, Existence and Truth. Look at a sunset, into the eyes of a baby, at acts of kindness or acts of heroism. What do you sense "within" You? Do you sense Wonder, Awe, Caring, Kindness, Personhood, Sacredness, Peace,

Stillness, Beauty, Acceptance, Joy, Strength, Courage, Compassion, Caring and/or Love? These Realities are within You. When you sense these Realities you are connected to your Spirit within. Your mind is connected to your Spirit. Your mind is connected to who You Are. Out there, the sunset is beautiful. But what is stirred within you? If you sense Love, Awe, Peace, Presence, Existence, Wonder, Beauty, Oneness, Gratitude or Sacredness; this is within You. This is You. This is who You Are. This is Truth. This is Being.

To make a choice between Truth and untruth it is necessary to see the lie. Lies are often unconscious. Compounding this fact is lack of awareness of and connection to the Truth. As a result, even if the lies are conscious, the lies are not recognized as lies. For example, if you believe you are worthless, you may be conscious of the fact you believe you are worthless; but if you are not aware of and connected to the Truth, you will not recognize that the belief "I am worthless" is a lie. Uncovering unconscious core lies is achieved through awareness of all the four facets. Uncovering unconscious core lies is a vital part of healing. These lies keep the Truth of who you Are hidden. Core lies cause pain, division, hatred, isolation, alienation, judgment, rejection, rage and fear.

Self is not the enemy. Your feelings are not the enemy. Your body is not the enemy. Your mind is not the enemy. Others are not the enemy. The outside is not the enemy. Unconscious core lies are the enemy. Lovelessness is the enemy. Lies about self, others and God are the enemy. Lack of awareness of Being is the enemy. Awareness of thoughts, emotions, body and Spirit is the answer to identifying these unconscious core lies. Thought awareness and emotional awareness are valuable keys to uncovering and recognizing unconscious core lies. Awareness of Being is at the same time awareness of Truth.

Emotional awareness is the mind learning to put words to felt emotions and inner sensations. Emotional awareness is the process of discovering and following the content of emotions and inner sensations. Emotional awareness begins first by just becoming aware of inner sensations and emotions felt within. The next steps are identifying individual emotions and eventually, following the content of these emotions and inner sensations. Emotions and inner sensations are picked up by the mind or intellect as a type of inner vibration in the body. At first the mind just senses "something" within. This something within is the inner sensation or inner vibration and it is felt in the body. Initially inner sensations are vague and seemingly indescribable. With time and patience you will begin to hear the content of inner sensations. You will hear the content by putting words to the emotions and inner sensations. These words will resonate with the emotions and inner sensations sensed in your body.

Emotions and inner sensations have a story to tell. Their story reveals your life's experiences and how the experiences have affected you. Within these experiences emotions and inner sensations reveal deeply held core lies believed as truth. These core lies about self are painful. Core lies about self are painful in three ways. First, believing a lie about self is painful. Lies hide the Truth. Not knowing the Truth of Being is painful. Lastly, core lies are closely associated and intertwined with unprocessed inner wounds of lovelessness and abuse. These inner wounds are painful. Abuse and unmet needs for Love are painful.

There are many different forms of lovelessness. Core lies are often deeply engrained as a result of lovelessness. This is especially the case when lovelessness is experienced as a child. Lovelessness includes abuse, rejection, hate, condemnation, negation, judgment, oppression, alienation, isolation and lack or absence of love. The more severe the abuse, rejection, hate and other forms of lovelessness, the more deeply engrained are the core lies. To dissolve these core lies requires continual reconnecting to the awareness of the Truth, the awareness of Spirit, the awareness of and identifying the core lie; as well as feeling and processing the pain of lovelessness and the pain from the core lie. Finally, to dissolve core lies requires taking a stand and choosing to believe the Truth. As loud as the core lie may proclaim its content, in the pain and in the face of the lies and untruth, make a conscious decision and choose the Truth. Choose to believe the Truth. Shift to the Truth. This process needs to be repeated many times over a period of time. Eventually the lie is dispelled by the Truth. Nurturing awareness of Being, connecting to Being and growing in Being dispels core lies. The loving Presence of others nurtures the awareness of and connection to the Reality of your Love, Presence and Existence within.

Nurture awareness of Truth. Nurture awareness of Being. Shift to Being. Connect to Being. Enter Being. The deepest Truth is...You Are. You Exist. You are Love and Truth. Say..."I Am". Enter..."I Am".

All unprocessed life experiences and beliefs are recorded and stored in the body waiting to reveal their content through emotions and inner sensations. Awareness of Spirit...of Being...of "I Am" through experiencing the deep inner Reality of Love, Truth, Existence, Presence, Peace, Oneness, Joy, Acceptance is the bedrock foundation required to confront untruth...to confront core lies about self. Awareness of Spirit and Truth dissolves evil. Light dispels darkness.

Mankind's deepest fear has at its root the most destructive core lie. This deep core lie negates Being and your very Existence. This deepest core lie creates intense fear, panic and anxiety. This core lie causes alienation, isolation, hatred, division, violence and destruction. This lie creates and affirms mankind's deepest fear. Mankind's deepest fear is the fear of non-Being. It is important to bring the lie at the root of this fear into the light. The deepest and most destructive core lie states...

"I am Not."

In this one lie; Being, Love, Life, Presence and Truth are negated. Existence is negated. Your Creator is negated. The "Truth" is the sword that will slay the dragon of untruth. The heart of the dragon is the lie "I am Not". The tip of the sword that can pierce the heart of the dragon is the Truth and the Reality...

"I Am."

Nurture awareness of and connection to...I Am. Come back to the Truth. Come back to Reality. Come back to...I Am. Enter...I Am. Choose...I Am.

You... Are.

You... Exist.

Say... "I Am".

ABOUT THE AUTHOR

 It is not uncommon for a person's life to unravel when faced with extreme stress or trauma. Dr. Dennis Murphy's primary mission in life is to help people find healing. Dennis's passion is to point people home to Being, so their thoughts and emotions align with Truth---the Truth of who they "really" Are. Dennis knows there is no single approach to healing, but he is convinced all forms of healing and all therapists can benefit from his insights. His books can dramatically shorten the journey to living a life of happiness, joy, peace and wholeness.

Dennis makes his home in the center of Canada and loves writing his books by the water on an island in northwestern Ontario. He's currently writing his latest books, *Heal Through the Power of Being and Daily Bread*. Long time healer and spiritual teacher Sister Theresa called his work "Transformational."

He especially hopes his books can free people from the dragon which creates so much depression, anxiety, addiction, division, isolation, negativity, loneliness, anger, hate, fear and pain. Free of the dragon, people can enjoy every precious moment and live an exceptional life.

Dr. Murphy has a six-year Doctor of Veterinary Medicine degree from the Western College of Veterinary Medicine in Canada. He belongs to the Manitoba Veterinary Medical Association and the Canadian Veterinary Medical Association. He graduated from Applied Counselling and Addictions Counselling after studying at the University of Manitoba and Brandon University. He studied Couples Therapy at the University of Winnipeg and General Counselling at the National College of Naturopathic Medicine. Dennis walks the walk. He has been committed to the work of personal growth and healing for over 30 years. To take advantage of his work, visit his website thenurturingdoctor.com and sign up to receive emails about his latest insights and new releases.

DISCLAIMER

The contents of this work are not intended as a substitute for consulting with your physician or other healthcare provider. The information in this book is not medical or psychological advice and should not be treated as such. If the issues of self harm or harm to others arise, consult a health care professional immediately. The author has a

Doctor of Veterinary Medicine degree and is not a human medical doctor, clinical psychologist or other licensed human health care professional. The author of this book does not dispense medical or psychological advice or prescribe the use of any technique as a form of treatment for physical, emotional, or medical problems without the advice of a physician, either directly or indirectly. You must not rely on the information in this book as an alternative to medical or psychological advice from your doctor or other professional healthcare provider. If you think you may be suffering from any medical or psychological condition you should seek immediate medical attention.

You should never delay seeking medical advice, disregard medical advice or discontinue medical treatment because of the information in this book. The intent of the author is to only offer information of a general nature to help you in your quest for spiritual well-being. In the event you use any of the information in this book for yourself, the author and the publisher assume no responsibility for your actions. While the publisher and author have used their best efforts in preparing this book, they make no representations or warranties with respect to the accuracy or completeness of the contents of this book and specifically disclaim all warranties, including without limitation warranties of merchantability or fitness for a particular purpose. No warranty may be created or extended by sales representatives or written sales materials. The author and publisher specifically disclaim all responsibility for any liability, loss or risk, personal or otherwise, which is incurred as a consequence, directly or indirectly, of the use and application of any of the contents of this book. The names and identifying details of people associated with events described in this book have been changed. Any similarity to actual persons is coincidental. Use of this book implies your acceptance of this disclaimer.

Made in the USA
Las Vegas, NV
04 October 2022

56507773R10075